Planning and Organising the SENCO Year

Planning and Organising the SENCO Year

Dot Constable

David Fulton Publishers Ltd
414 Chiswick High Road, London W4 5TF

www.fultonpublishers.co.uk

First published in Great Britain in 2002 by David Fulton Publishers

British Library Cataloguing in Publication Data
A catalogue record for this book is available from the British Library.

ISBN 1-85346-802-9

Typeset by Elite Typesetting Techniques, Eastleigh, Hampshire
Printed and bound in Great Britain

Contents

Acknowledgements

While writing this book many faces have flashed across my mind of those children who have in some way or other made my life in schools special. Working in the field of special educational needs (SEN) for me has always been a delight. I have loved the working relationships created and have derived immeasurable pleasure from watching many of the children I have taught achieve their potential. As I worked through the section on individual education plans (IEPs), I recalled some of the wonderful characters whose profiles and targets I had written and whose reviews had brought much more than a smile to my face. I can assure you that they were by no means all angelic but it seems to me that somehow they always had the ability, at the point of my despair, to come up trumps. Their sense of humour, their smiles of appreciation, their wonderful views on life would somehow rescue the moment. These relationships, however, would never have been possible without the support and help of other colleagues to whom I am eternally grateful. I cannot personally thank all of the people who have supported me over the years, but I would like to take this opportunity to say thank you to those who have had a direct impact upon this book.

Jean Swift

Many of the ideas contained in the book have been shared and developed with others, but in particular I would like to thank Jean Swift who produced the Spelling Progression Checklist and who provided the basics for the development of the SEN Monitoring Form. Jean is a fervent supporter of pupils who have SEN and she has most definitely had an impact on the lives of many of them.

Sheila Atherden

I would also like to take this opportunity to thank Sheila Atherden for her efforts in proof-reading parts of the book. Sheila is a member of the Sandwell LEA Support Services who, like myself, has a passion for enhancing a positive profile of SEN. Her personality and love of life are transcended into her work and she is a wonderful ambassador for the cause.

Lynda Wood

During the course of the book you will become aware of the importance I place on the SENCO having an administrative assistant. I can say it is most definitely worthwhile. My administrative assistant, Lynda Wood, was brilliant. She was efficient, effective, gave support to both staff and children and most importantly, she made me laugh! Thank you, Lynda.

Margaret Roberts

Finally, my biggest vote of thanks goes out to Margaret Roberts, who throughout the project has kept me buoyant and cheerful. Margaret is a colleague whose capacity for hard work, sense of fairness, professional dedication and ability to keep everyone smiling in the face of adversity have always been an inspiration to me. I am eternally grateful to her for her help and guidance throughout and for the gift of her valuable time to proof-read this book. Thank you, Margaret – I couldn't have done it without you.

Dedication

I would like to dedicate this book to the staff and children of Churchfields High School, West Bromwich, for whom I shall always keep a special place in my heart. Sadly the school closed its doors forever on 31 August 2001 and we all went our separate ways. To all of you I would like to say – thank you for 'the way we were'.

Introduction: the need for planning and organisation

What does the job entail?

The role of the special educational needs coordinator (SENCO) is clearly defined in the Code of Practice (Department for Education and Employment (DfEE) 1994a; Department for Education and Skills (DfES) 2001). The Code suggests that under the auspices of the head teacher and governing body, the designated person in charge of SEN may have responsibility for:

- The school's SEN policy documentation and its implementation.
- Liaising, advising and supporting colleagues.
- Managing the school's SEN team.
- Organisation and provision for pupils who are designated as having SEN.
- Appropriate record-keeping.
- Liaising and working with parents.
- In-service training of staff.
- Multi-agency liaison.

What the Code does not give, however, is appropriate advice and guidance on how to manage the workload. This surely poses the question: is it humanly possible for one person to carry out this role?

The answer to this question is implicit in the title of the job – special educational needs coordinator. By definition, a coordinator is someone who organises people or things to work properly together. The SENCO's role is one of managing the coordination in respect of the educational provision for pupils with SEN. This I truly believe is possible, but it is dependent on good systems and effective strategies and resourcing.

The need for planning and organisation

Forward planning and good organisational skills are crucial if SENCOs are to be able to carry out the numerous duties and tasks required of them. They are often expected to provide quick solutions to a number of problems while at the same time delivering the curriculum, writing individual education plans (IEPs), completing paperwork, running reviews, attending meetings, liaising with outside agencies ... need I go on? The solution to the problem lies in whole-school involvement. Systems need to be designed, ideas shared, colleagues educated and responsibilities delegated if the provision for SEN in mainstream schools is to be a manageable task for the SENCO.

With this in mind, and in light of the statutory duties on local education authorities (LEAs) and schools as laid out in the Revised Code of Practice (DfES 2001) and the Special Educational Needs and Disability Act 2001 (HMSO 2001), this publication was put together to share ideas, strategies and mechanisms to provide equality of opportunity for pupils with SEN in mainstream schools. The main objective is to support colleagues in a practical way towards achieving SEN provision that is cost effective, workable but, most importantly to the SENCO, manageable. The starting point is a yearly planner which came about from my own desire to be able to 'spread the workload' across the academic year. Following on from this it is hoped that the information and ideas contained in the remaining chapters will support the reader in a variety of ways, irrespective of their background.

This publication will be of interest to:

- Newly appointed SENCOs.
- SENCOs in post.
- Senior management teams (SMTs).
- SEN link governors/governing bodies.
- Teachers undergoing SENCO training.
- Those involved in the training of SENCOs.
- LEA (SEN advisor/support services).

The book has been designed for ease of reference in the hope that it will be used, as intended, as a working document for all those who are involved in the provision for pupils who have SEN.

1 A yearly planner

Where it all started

Being a SENCO is one of the most difficult positions of responsibility assigned to any one person in a school. The job requires endless energy with continuing demands from managers, teachers, governors, LEAs, parents – not forgetting the children! The list of tasks (which seems to duplicate in size overnight) is truly never-ending.

I usually wonder what madness possesses colleagues to take on such a role, but I guarantee that anyone who talks to a SENCO will quickly realise that they are very devoted to the children in their care and often passionate in their defence when fighting for equality of opportunity. They will probably be the first to admit that they do not like the administration, the bureaucracy, the endless sheets of paper to be completed; but what they do like is the look on the children's faces when they transcend through the learning block, develop a new skill, begin to enjoy school once again and achieve the impossible. The point is that SENCOs feel they are truly able to make a difference and have an impact.

I am sure that what most SENCOs would appreciate would be a reduction of the administrative and managerial pressures of the role, which could in turn alleviate some of the stresses that most of them encounter and enable them to devote more time to the children in their care. It is from a personal point of view that I take up the case. At a poignant time in my career when I was not only a SENCO but also a senior teacher (with added whole-school responsibilities), I decided the time had come to consider my effectiveness. I was at that time, for want of a better term, 'treading water'. On many occasions I felt that my head was most definitely below rather than above the water line, and my contact time with the children was being eroded. Time to evaluate!

I decided that the two areas in need of the greatest consideration were time management and delegation of duties. It soon became evident that in respect of the SENCO's role, there was a need for a system that could be organised in a logical order, planned well ahead and ultimately designed to avoid pressure points during the year. This was the key. There were too many occasions during the year where task overload was common. I hit on the idea of producing a yearly planner whereby the tasks could, I hoped, be spread out, giving me at least a fighting chance of survival. Once developed, the second area – the delegation of roles/jobs – could then be considered.

With the two goals in mind I set about developing the ideas.

The yearly planner

The first task was to put together a list of all the jobs that had to be carried out during the year. These were as follows:

- Pupil assessment – screen tests and individual diagnostic tests.
- SEN register – updating of the register.
- IEPs – writing/updating.
- Preparation for reviews – initiation and collation of required paperwork.
- The review itself – the meeting.
- Post-review action – initiating action required and completion of relevant paperwork.
- Meetings with outside agencies with regard to pupils with SEN or school support for staff.
- Organisation/evaluation of the school's support for pupils with SEN.
- Monitoring/evaluation/action in respect of SEN provision.
- SEN policy documentation review.
- Reports to governors.
- In-service training and education (INSET).

The next task was to break down each one further. For example, the annual reviews for statemented pupils were organised in year groups and placed at appropriate times of the year, i.e. Year 9 was put into February (prior to option choices) and Year 7 into December (to evaluate the effectiveness of Key Stage 2 to Key Stage 3 transfer). By going through this process with all the points on the list, it provided an extensive list of all the tasks to be completed.

From the outset I felt this part of the job was probably going to be the most arduous. I decided upon the best plan of attack – the use of a spreadsheet. This would enable all of the information required to be put in any order and then, by allocating times of the year, the computer could be used to sort and re-sort the information. Ultimately the finished product would be a calendar of events in date order and it would then be possible to see at a glance where overloads were likely to occur. Rearranging the list to even out the workload would then become relatively easy.

By completing it in this way the task was nowhere near as difficult as I expected. Although it required an input of time, once completed it only needed minor alterations each year. The final product (see Fig. 1.1) meant that I could see immediately what lay ahead and be well prepared.

Getting help

The next step was to look for areas where delegation would be possible. There were certain aspects of the job that could be done far more quickly and efficiently by a competent typist – someone who could send out the paperwork for reviews, collate the relevant information, update the SEN register – and indeed probably do far more. This, however, had implications in respect of funding. As one would expect, the person taking on such tasks would probably like to be paid! This part of the plan needed to be discussed at senior management level to ascertain whether it was viable. After putting a very powerful case on value for money, it was agreed that an average of 2.5 hours per week secretarial time would be allocated to SEN tasks which were as follows:

- In liaison with the SENCO, update of the computerised SEN register as and when required and issue to all staff.
- In liaison with the SENCO and SEN teachers, type/update IEPs and have responsibility for issuing to staff.
- Issue, collect and collate all information for pupil reviews and have ready for the SENCO one week prior to the review itself.
- Send out all information and invitations to identified people involved in the review and inform the SENCO of acceptances/apologies received.
- Type up details of pupil reviews and issue to named people.
- Complete typed reports/information as and when requested by the SENCO.

It was agreed from the outset that the time allocated could fluctuate from week to week dependent on need, but that it would ultimately average out to the agreed hours. The system was to be monitored for effectiveness and was to be re-evaluated at the end of the year.

The results of the evaluation were most definitely favourable. There was a marked improvement in the efficiency and effectiveness of the planning, paperwork and administration. Well-produced, accurate information was at hand thanks to the administrative assistant. Noticeably more quality time had become available for working with the children.

The new system was retained and proved to be invaluable. I would openly encourage all SENCOs to produce their own yearly calendar and, where at all possible, obtain secretarial support. If head teachers use the excuse that the school does not have sufficient funds, ask them to evaluate the cost effectiveness of their current system. The ultimate aim of any SEN provision within a school must surely be 'best value'.

Where to now?

It is now time to investigate further some of the areas outlined in the planner where sharing ideas may provide further support to SENCOs, their schools and, indeed, beyond. Essentially the starting point must be the revised Code of Practice (DfES 2001) and the subsequent policy documentation. There is a definite need to understand the requirements of both in order to facilitate the development of effective practice in SEN provision.

Job	Task	Completed by
Allocation of support – Term 1	Meeting with support staff to discuss allocation of pupil support	15 September
Annual governors' report	Working with SEN governor to produce report for inclusion in annual report to parents	17 September
Yr 7 spelling tests	Screen test whole of Yr 7	20 September
IEP distribution	All IEPs for Yr 8 and above updated and issued to staff	22 September
Term 1 planning meeting with outside agencies	Meeting with external support services to discuss case loads and plan Autumn term work	30 September
Yr 7 spelling tests	Marked and individual pupils identified for further assessment	30 September
CATS (NFER)	Pupils to take tests	1 October
SEN register update	Yr 7 pupils added to SEN register, update, printed and issued to staff	10 October
Yr 7 diagnostic assessment and IEPs	Identified pupils begin individualised diagnostic testing and IEPs written and distributed	31 October
CATS (NFER)	Tests marked and information issued to staff	31 October
Yr 7 statement reviews preparation	Paperwork issued to all concerned	1 December
SEN governor update	SEN governor monitoring visit	4 December
Yr 7 statement reviews	Review to take place and paperwork forwarded to LEA SEN section. Subsequent action to be initiated	17 December
Allocation of support – Term 2	Meeting with support staff to discuss allocation of pupil support	7 January
IEP distribution	Amended IEPs printed and distributed to staff	8 January
SEN register update	SEN register updated and information disseminated to staff	15 January
Term 2 planning meeting with outside agencies	Meeting with external support services to discuss case loads and plan Spring term work	18 January
Yr 9 statement reviews preparation	Paperwork issued to all concerned	25 January
Yr 11 stage 2/3 review	Review to take place at Yr 11 parents' evening and paperwork completed. Subsequent action to be initiated	31 January
Yr 9 stage 2/3 review	Review to take place at Yr 9 parents' evening and paperwork completed. Subsequent action to be initiated	31 January
Yr 9 statement reviews	Review to take place and paperwork forwarded to LEA SEN section. Subsequent action to be initiated	18 February
SEN governor update	SEN governor monitoring visit	20 February
Yr 10 stage 2/3 review	Review to take place at Yr 10 parents' evening and paperwork completed. Subsequent action to be initiated	28 February

continued

Job	Task	Completed by
Yr 8 statement reviews preparation	Paperwork issued to all concerned	6 March
Yr 8 statement reviews	Review to take place and paperwork forwarded to LEA SEN section. Subsequent action to be initiated	25 March
Yr 11 statement reviews preparation	Paperwork issued to all concerned	25 March
SATS/Yr 11 exams	Pupils needing support in external tests/exams identified and programme of support planned	31 March
Allocation of support – Term 3	Meeting with support staff to discuss allocation of pupil support	26 April
Yr 8 stage 2/3 review	Review to take place at Yr 8 parents' evening and paperwork completed. Subsequent action to be initiated	30 April
Yr 7 stage 2/3 review	Review to take place at Yr 7 parents' evening and paperwork completed . Subsequent action to be initiated	30 April
Term 3 planning meeting with outside agencies	Meeting with external support services to discuss case loads and plan Summer term work	6 May
Yr 11 statement reviews	Review to take place and paperwork forwarded to LEA SEN section. Subsequent action to be initiated	7 May
Yr 10 statement reviews preparation	Paperwork issued to all concerned	12 June
Yr 10 statement reviews	Review to take place and paperwork forwarded to LEA SEN section. Subsequent action to be initiated	26 June
Literacy/reading assessment Yr 6	Yr 6 to complete assessments during school visits	30 June
SEN governor update	SEN governor monitoring visit	7 July
Literacy/reading assessment Yr 6	To be marked, graphed and available to head of year	10 July
SEN register update	Admin assistant updates as and when pupils are moved on register	Ongoing
IEP distribution	Interim updates of IEPs where alterations are required	Ongoing
SEN monitoring	Lesson monitoring to evaluate effectiveness of SEN provision	Ongoing
Yr 7 –11 stage 2/3 reviews	Additional reviews to take place by SEN staff at designated/appointed times. Subsequent action to be initiated	Ongoing
Allocation of pupil support	Minor changes as and when required to allocation of pupil support	Ongoing
In-service training	Organised according to individual and school needs	Ongoing

Figure 1.1 The yearly planner

2 Special educational needs – the Code of Practice

Background: 1994–2002

The Code of Practice came into effect in 1994 (DfEE 1994a). It set out regulations and statutory duties that LEAs and schools had to consider when looking at the educational provision for pupils who had identified SEN.

It certainly had a major impact. Schools and LEAs had to radically rethink the way in which they catered for such pupils. Systems had to be devised, regulations put in place, educational provision re-evaluated. It culminated in a whole new way of thinking and working. For the first time schools were introduced to a new terminology, that of SENCO, the special educational needs coordinator – the person in school who, for the first few years, was to take the full weight of this mammoth task squarely on their shoulders.

From the outset, the burden of the paperwork rapidly became apparent. All around the country people were devising ways of coping with what seemed to be an insurmountable task – designing IEPs, producing proformas, recording and reporting, writing policy documentation, etc. It was a time when, for the first time, the SENCO became aware of the size and extent of the role and the amount of work that lay ahead. It soon became obvious that although the provision for children with SEN improved, it was too often bogged down in bureaucracy and therefore not cost effective. There was a definite need for this situation to be addressed.

The move towards a rethink came about in 1997 when the Green Paper, *Excellence for All Children: Meeting Special Educational Needs* (DfEE 1997) set out the government's agenda for improving the achievements of children with SEN. The then Secretary of State for Education and Employment, the Rt. Hon. David Blunkett MP, stated in his opening comments in the document the need for reappraisal, the need to build on good practice and the need for a change in the law.

Following on from this, *Meeting Special Educational Needs: A Programme of Action* (DfEE 1998) was published, which, as its title implies, set out the actions to be taken towards achieving the government's objectives. In relation to the Code of Practice, Section 2, Improving the SEN Framework, set out the planned changes. A lengthy consultation process followed. Conferences, meetings and discussions were held to seek the views of a wide range of people with an interest in SEN, including those of professionals and parents. The result of this process was the revised Code of Practice that came into effect in January 2002 (DfES 2001).

What does the revised Code offer?

As the document states in the Introduction, 'The SEN Code of Practice provides practical advice to Local Education Authorities, maintained schools, early education settings and others carrying out their statutory duties to identify, assess and make provision for children with special educational needs'. It is set out in 10 chapters (Fig. 2.1) and provides, as stated in Chapter 1 (Principles and Policies), 'guidance on policies and procedures aimed at enabling pupils with special educational needs (SEN) to reach their full potential, to be included fully in their school communities and make successful transition to adulthood'.

The layout is clear and relatively easy to access giving the reader an opportunity to use it as a reference document when planning, organising or evaluating SEN provision. In relation to this, the Introduction to the Code states its importance in helping schools and LEAs in their efforts to achieve best value. Having taken into account experiences of schools and LEAs in using the original Code, developments in education since 1994 and the new rights and duties introduced by the Special Educational Needs and Disability Act 2001 (HMSO 2001) and regulations, it is hoped the resulting action will be less bureaucratic, more efficient in terms of resourcing and more effective in achieving high standards for those children with SEN.

Figure 2.2 illustrates the major changes to the original Code. Eight identified points show the areas where new initiatives and altered perspectives require careful consideration. This is of paramount importance if the intention of the revised Code is to be achieved: 'a more efficient, cost-effective, better resourced system for special educational needs provision'.

What are the implications for schools?

As for all systems and educational provision within schools there must be a continuous cycle of review, evaluation and further planning. The clock must never stand still as the needs of children are ever changing. Our goal must always be to provide an educational system within each school that caters for all, gives equal opportunity to all and is truly inclusive.

In light of the revised Code of Practice this cycle should continue with the necessary changes being implicit in the forward planning. Whether it be the year 2002 or 2022, there will always be children with SEN. The success or failure of schools in respect of this centre around whole-school involvement. It is not just the SENCO's responsibility – it is equally the responsibility of governors, head teachers, teachers and support staff alike to ensure that all children are effectively catered for. As one would expect, there are defined

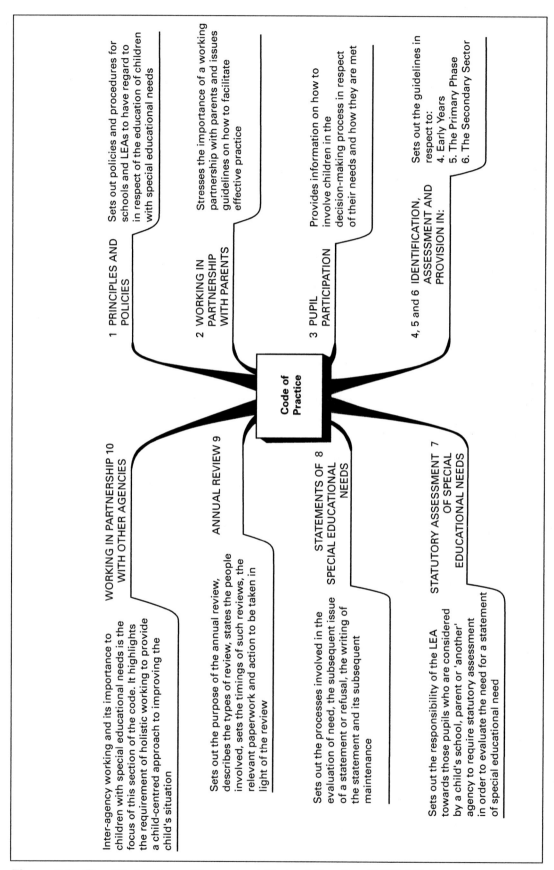

Figure 2.1 The 10 chapters of the revised Code of Practice (DfES 2001)

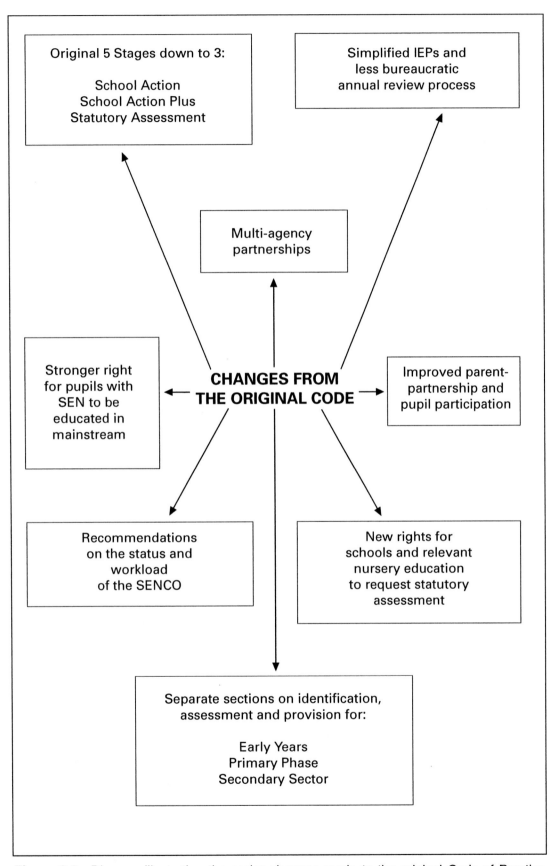

Figure 2.2 Diagram illustrating the major changes made to the original Code of Practice (DfEE 1994a)

areas within the Code where particular roles are identified which the SENCO may have responsibility for as a manager, e.g. managing the SEN team of teachers and learning support assistants (LSAs), however, the wider implications still come back to whole-school involvement.

Now for reality

Yes, I know, if you are a SENCO, having read the previous paragraph you are now ready to close the book and give up! You are thinking – 'what on earth does this maniac think she is talking about?' I can see your faces now as you visualise a particular teacher who comes up with such phrases as:

- Yeah – but (s)he is one of yours!
- What am I expected to do if (s)he can't read or write?
- How can I be expected to teach him/her when I've got a class full?
- They shouldn't be in this school!
- How do you expect me to do this?

I'm sure if I asked for further suggestions that there would be enough to write a book. There is, however, a point to all of this and that is a message to all head teachers and school governors – you have a vital role to play in supporting the SENCO in the discharge of their duties, in particular in relation to whole-school issues. Now read on!

Implementing the Code

The remaining chapters of this book aim to look at identifiable areas from within the Code, provide a basic understanding of the requirements within and then strive to provide simplistic, effective and manageable suggestions for achieving a realistic workload.

   If these aims are achieved, the ultimate goal will have been met – to lessen the burden of bureaucracy while at the same time retaining (or indeed enhancing) good quality SEN provision.

3 Proactive policies

The first thought that came to mind at the outset of writing this chapter was the chicken and egg syndrome. What comes first, policy or practice? Do you write the policy and expect people to follow it or do you facilitate good practice first and then put pen to paper?

For those of us who can – remember the days at the outset of the Office for Standards in Education (Ofsted)? Schools were writing policies at a great rate of knots prior to their first official inspection under the new regulations. Truckloads of materials were parcelled and packaged to go off to the inspectors. But, of all the policies sent, how many staff knew what was in each one? How many of those selfsame staff had been involved in the development of them? The answer, I guess, would be very few. However, ask them if they knew how the school was organised, what the rules and regulations were and what actions were needed in response to a wide variety of issues and they would probably have replied readily to the questions posed.

My point? We spent far too much time writing elaborate documentation when the actions for effective provision were already in place. What was needed was a practical approach whereby:

- current practice was notated
- effectiveness was evaluated
- staff were consulted
- due regard was given to DfEE/LEA and school directives
- from this amendments were made where necessary
- and finally a concise, usable document was written.

This action is as applicable today as it would have been then. Schools still need to look at their policies annually and amend where necessary if they wish to have effective working documents in place. The title of this chapter therefore has a very important point to make because:

A policy needs to be a working document which is of use to its writers, its users and its readers. It must be proactive and not just written to meet the requirements of inspection.

11

So, back to the chicken or the egg. I feel there is a simplistic way to solve this problem – a 'two-pronged' attack. It must take into account both policy and practice at the same time. How can this be achieved you might ask. Well, the starting point should be the DfEE Circular 6/94, *The Organisation of Special Educational Provision* (DfEE 1994b).

This document sets out in Part 1 the main elements needed for an SEN policy. Taking each point in turn one can consider what the school needs to cover in respect of the Circular while at the same time evaluating current practice. From this adjustments or amendments can be made in order to achieve successful provision for SEN.

Statutory Instrument 1999 No.2506 and Circular 6/94

Statutory Instrument 1999 No.2506, which was laid before parliament on 8 September 1999 and came into force on 1 October 1999, sets out the information required about a school's SEN provision (Regulation 3 (1)). It does, however, only encompass the basic guidelines and is not as detailed as Circular 6/94 (which followed the 1993 Education Act). This particular document offers a more comprehensive picture of what is required and therefore, in light of this, this chapter is based around that guidance.

The following information is taken from Circular 6/94 (Part 1, School's SEN Policies) with regard to SEN policy documentation. It sets out the areas that ought to be included in any policy.

a. *The school's objectives in making provision for pupils with special educational needs: Schedule 1:1 of the Education (Special Educational Needs) (Information) Regulations 1994*

The following points need to be considered when producing the objectives:

- Regard must be given to the Education Acts and related documentation in respect of SEN.
- They should reflect the LEA educational development policy and all policy documentation which has regard to SEN.
- They should be in line with whole-school aims as laid down in whole-school policy documentation.
- They should lay down the school's beliefs in respect of SEN.

b. *The person responsible for co-ordinating the day-to-day provision of education for pupils with special educational needs (or the SEN co-ordinator): Schedule 1:2*

The policy should identify the named person in the school.

c. *Arrangements for co-ordinating provision for pupils with special educational needs: Schedule 1:3*

The SENCO's list of duties assigned to them in line with the Code of Practice should be identified.

d. *Admissions arrangements for pupils with special educational needs but without a statement: Schedule 1:4*

A statement should be included that outlines the admission arrangements of the school. Within this statement, the following needs to be considered:

- Any criteria/rules laid down for admissions, for example, entrance examinations, LEA agreements.
- Any identified reasons which give priority to particular individuals/groups i.e. such as a specialism for children with hearing impairment or other SEN.
- It should list the criteria used for such circumstances.
- It should identify if the LEA gives priority to admitting particular identified groups. (NB 'The number of places allocated under special criteria for educational reasons should not exceed 10% of the total intake.')

Warning: schools must, in the light of the Special Educational Needs and Disability Act 2001 (HMSO 2001), ensure that their admissions policy is able to live up to scrutiny in respect of unlawful discrimination against disabled pupils.

Remember, any decisions made must be justifiable in the eyes of the law!

e. *Any SEN specialism and any special units: Schedule 1:5*

This section **must describe any particular special educational need of which the school has particular experience and in which it has developed some expertise** and it should include:

- The expertise of staff in relation to SEN.
- The specialist resources available.
- A brief outline of curricular arrangements and identifiable support for all pupils with SEN.
- A description of any special unit placed within a mainstream school.

f. *Facilities for pupils with special educational needs: Schedule 1:6*

It should describe any particular arrangements, fixtures, fittings etc. that the school has for providing appropriate access to the school and its curriculum.

g. *Resources: Schedule 1:7*

This section **must describe the principles governing the school's allocation of resources to and among pupils with SEN** and should identify arrangements for the resourcing of SEN provision. In order for schools to provide appropriate information in relation to best value, the following details should be included:

- Annual SEN budget allocation.
- Allocation of resources to pupils who have SEN.
- Annual analysis on value for money.
- Future planning in relation to the above.

h. *Identification, assessment and provision: Schedule 1:8*

This section of the document **must outline the school's systems for dealing with the identification, assessment, record-keeping and review for all pupils who may have an SEN.** It should also include information on School Action, School Action Plus and statutory assessment in relation to provision at each stage.

i. *Access to the curriculum: Schedule 1:9*

The policy must explain how the school will provide pupils with SEN with access to a balanced and broadly based curriculum, including the National Curriculum. Here the policy should outline the types of provision in place that enable all pupils to access the curriculum. This may include for example:

- In-class support.
- Small teaching groups.
- Specialised teaching programmes.
- Specialist equipment/resources.
- Specialised staff i.e. speech therapist.
- Support staff.

j. *Integration arrangements: Schedule 1:10*

Here, the schedule highlights the fact that governing bodies **must ensure that pupils with SEN join in the activities of the school together with pupils who do not have SEN.** In light of recent legislation I would suggest this section is not included but rather that in all other sections regard is given to the issue of inclusion. Where schools have policy documentation that refers to inclusion, particular reference must be made to it. Inclusion should be intrinsic throughout the SEN policy.

k. *Evaluating success: Schedule 1:11*

This part of the documentation **must set out systems for the evaluation of the effectiveness of the implementation of the SEN policy.** As governors are responsible for the school's SEN provision it would seem logical that part of the evaluation process would include their annual report to parents.

l. *Any arrangements for the treatment of complaints: Schedule 1:12*

Emphasis should be placed on the importance of parent partnership. Information contained in this part of the document should identify particular points of contact where, if the parent feels the need to put forward a complaint, they are able to do so.

m. *SEN in-service training for staff: Schedule 1:13*

This must relate to the needs of the school and the needs of individual/whole-school staff and should refer to the school's professional development policy/plans.

n. *External support services: Schedule 1:14*

A list should be provided of all external agencies the school is in contact with or whom they may need to contact.

o. *Partnership with parents: Schedule 1:15*

A brief statement should be written to establish the school's arrangements for working closely with parents. It may relate to other documents within school that have regard to this partnership. There should also be information on how they are given access to information and support in respect of their child.

p. *Links with other schools, including special schools, and arrangements for transition between schools and beyond school: Schedule 1:16*

A summary of the school's links with other schools should take into account mainstream/special and cross-phase links and should name in each case the link person.

q. *Links with the health services, social services and any voluntary organisations: Schedule 1:17*

In light of the revised Code of Practice 2001, this should be included in the section on external agencies.

All of the above schedules need consideration but take note, where the word **must** is evident it is purposely highlighted to endorse the fact that there is a statutory requirement laid down in each particular case.

So, now that you have all of the information required to consider an SEN policy what do you do next?

Don't panic

Remember that the most important part of the equation is what is happening in reality – irrespective of the paperwork. If your practice is successful, writing the document is easy because you are writing about what you do (if it isn't, start by evaluating what changes are needed to make it successful). Take heed and keep the document as short as possible (you will find a sample policy document at the end of this chapter).

Once the document is drafted take it through a consultation process in order to ensure that on final completion its users are able to feel ownership towards it. (This may be done by trialling through practice and amending after feedback and evaluation.)

If you are amending an existing document, still go through the process of involving others by informal discussions. The policy document should be reviewed each year (and amendments made where necessary) prior to the governors' reporting to parents. This is part of the school's evaluation of effectiveness of SEN provision.

Finally, **remember** the document needs to be concise and accessible to its audience so, for those of you who have policy documents that are heavy enough to press flowers between – think again! They are not being read, they are a nightmare to evaluate each year and they are more often than not of very little use to anyone. If yours is one of those think about the rewrite; it may be a painful experience but in the long term it will definitely be a time-saver.

SAMPLE POLICY

The following document is intended as an exemplar and may be adjusted according to need. It is hoped that it will be of use across all phases. At the end of some of the paragraphs/items, information will appear in italic print to provide points of consideration or suggestions for adaptation.

SCHOOL

SPECIAL EDUCATIONAL NEEDS POLICY

Date of the Policy: (Insert original date of first policy)

The Special Needs Policy takes careful account of the Education Act 1996, the Code of Practice 2001, the Special Educational Needs and Disability Act 2001, the policy of the Local Education Authority and the aims of the school as outlined in school documentation.

All children have skills, talents and abilities and as a school we have a responsibility to develop these to the full. We believe that:

All children are entitled to a relevant and worthwhile education designed to enable individual pupils to participate fully in society and to contribute to and benefit from it.

Pupils who have special educational needs should be supported wherever necessary to achieve full access to the whole-school curriculum. This will need to be facilitated through a range of access technologies including skilled staff, specialist equipment and resources.

Pupils should have special programmes designed to maximise opportunities for independent living in preparation for life after school, including preparation for work or continuing education.

With regard to these beliefs, the following document outlines the provision the school endeavours to achieve.

THE MANAGEMENT OF SEN

The SEN Coordinator is —————————— and (s)he has the responsibility for the day-to-day operation of the SEN policy.

The SEN Coordinator will:

a) Oversee the running of the provision for pupils with special educational needs including general class, small group and individual pupil support.

b) Organise and manage the work of the school's Learning Support Assistants (SEN support teachers).

c) Maintain the school's Special Needs Register and all the required documentation.

d) Keep records on pupils who have special educational needs and ensure their progress is regularly monitored and reviewed.

e) Liaise with teachers, parents and external agencies.

f) Ensure annual reviews for statemented pupils are completed.

g) Organise meetings as appropriate with designated teachers at regular intervals in respect of special needs issues.

h) Regularly review and monitor SEN provision within the school.

i) Take part in formal meetings with external agencies regarding individual pupils to be assessed.

j) Liaise with the pastoral team regarding pupils on the SEN Register (secondary schools).

k) Liaise with Literacy Co-Coordinator, Numeracy Co-Coordinator, class teachers/subject departments/teachers to ensure the needs of pupils with special educational needs are met throughout all the subjects of the curriculum.

l) In line with the school's professional development programme/policy provide access to in-service training to meet the needs of the school and individual members of staff.

m) Produce termly reports to the designated SEN governor and an annual report for the 'Governors' Report to Parents'.

ADMISSION ARRANGEMENTS

The school adheres to the admission policy of the LEA and therefore has no special provision under admission arrangements for limiting or promoting access for pupils with special needs who are without statements. It does, however, endeavour to provide appropriate support for pupils with a range of special educational needs.

Or

(continued from above) In addition to this the school has specialist provision for —————————— and will therefore have placements for (number) pupils to be enrolled in this provision at any one time. Pupils who have such identified needs will be given consideration under the school's and LEA's admission policies.

SEN SPECIALISMS

The school accommodates provision for pupils who experience difficulties in:

- Communication and interaction
- Cognition and learning
- Behaviour, emotional and social development
- Sensory and/or physical
- Medical conditions

(You may wish to add – in particular, the school caters for pupils who have _____ (identify specific need))

ACCESS FOR THE DISABLED

The school has full access for disabled pupils.

Or

The school has provided some access for disabled pupils through ramped access to particular buildings and toilet facilities within those areas (if in one designated area, state where that is). The needs of the pupil will be taken into account when considering timetabling arrangements in order to ensure full access to the curriculum is available.

SPECIAL EDUCATIONAL NEEDS BUDGET ALLOCATION AND ANALYSIS IN RELATION TO THE DELIVERY OF SEN SUPPORT

With regard to the annual allocated budget as set out in LEA documentation and in line with the aims and beliefs of this policy document, the following information outlines the basis on which the school plans for the delivery of SEN support.

Annual Budget Allocation

The annual allocation of budget for special educational needs for the year is £_____

This figure is as outlined in the LEA's published budget figures for the school's SEN spending for the academic year _____ to _____

At this point, include details of the LEA's criteria and information sent out to the school in respect of the SEN budget.

Allocation of Resources to Pupils with SEN

The following information outlines the current allocation of resources with respective costings for each:

Staffing for delivery of SEN programmes of work

	Give costing	Give % of FTE
Learning Support Assistants	Give costing	Give % of FTE
Administrative Support	Give costing	Give % of FTE
Resources (annual capitation) for the SEN dept		Give costing
Resources (part of annual capitation) for other departments/areas of responsibility in respect of SEN		Give costing
Other___(include any other items which are costed against SEN)		Give costing

TOTAL COSTING   £_____

If SEN funding is higher than the incoming allocated budget, there will be a need to state the amount of overspend and from where it is being funded.

*** Note: I would expect to update this section of the policy documentation on receipt of the annual budget allocation. This would be an opportune time to complete the annual revision/evaluation of the document.**

Analysis of Best Value

The SENCO and the school management team use both quantitative and qualitative analysis in the evaluation of SEN provision. The following criteria are used to establish best value:

- Pupils on SEN register having made varying degrees of progress according to staff records.
- Annual reading, spelling and diagnostic assessments demonstrate an individual's progress.
- Comparative data from standardised tests (*name the tests*) are used as guidelines for assessing the pupil's ability in working to their full potential.
- By lesson observation feedback to assess suitability of curriculum materials, delivery and use of support allocated for pupils with special educational needs.
- Monitoring of SEN provision via a range of proformas to gather information on pupils, staffing and systems in place.

Future Planning

Future planning on SEN takes place in accordance with:

- Ongoing evaluation of best value
- Annual SEN budget allowance
- Ongoing LEA and government directives

IDENTIFICATION, ASSESSMENT, RECORD-KEEPING AND REVIEW

School Action

Identification

The identification would be with regard to the information as outlined in the Code of Practice: 'The triggers for intervention through *School Action* could be the teachers or others' concern, underpinned by evidence, about a child who despite receiving differentiated learning opportunities:

- Makes little or no progress even when teaching approaches are targeted particularly in a child's identified areas of weakness
- Shows signs of difficulty in developing literacy or mathematics skills which result in poor attainment in some curriculum areas
- Presents persistent emotional or behavioural difficulties which are not ameliorated by the behaviour management techniques usually employed in the school
- Has sensory or physical problems, and continues to make little or no progress despite the provision of specialist equipment
- Has communication and/or interaction difficulties, and continues to make little or no progress despite the provision of a differentiated curriculum'

The gathering of information in respect of identifying the pupil's special educational needs may be via:

1. Liaison with teachers.
2. Liaison with pre-school provision/Infant School(s)/Junior School(s). (*choose as appropriate*)
3. Liaison with parents by school parents' meetings and individual contact : school–parent/parent–school.
4. Liaison with external agencies where pupils may have been known to their service.

Assessment of Needs

1. Information from feeder schools initially.
2. Whole-school screen assessments. (*Name the tests used by the school e.g. NFER CATS*)
3. SEN screen test(s). (*Name the tests used by the school e.g. SPOONCER Literacy Assessment*)
4. Diagnostic assessment of individuals highlighted from the above three areas.

5. Class teacher/subject area comments and analysis of progress registered through:
    i) Class teacher/departmental targets
    ii) Class teacher/departmental ongoing marking/assessment
    iii) Pupil reviews
    iv) Pupil reports
6. Pupils referred by class/subject teachers as giving cause for concern and therefore meriting assessment and possible inclusion on SEN register.
7. Ongoing assessment, review and record-keeping of pupils in line with the school's organisation of the Code of Practice.

Process for Action, Record-Keeping and Review

1. Upon referral to the SENCO, an assessment of the pupil is undertaken to identify the nature of the need and the severity.
2. Appropriate information is gathered from staff teaching the pupil, the tutor and any other teacher who is deemed to have a valuable input.
3. Discussion takes place with parents to gather appropriate/relevant information on the child.
4. Individual Education Plan:
    From the collated information, the SENCO discusses the child's needs with the child and parents and, where appropriate, upon agreement, issues IEP No.1 to the staff, parents and child. The support to be provided for the child will be indicated on the IEP. (Where there is deemed to be no SEN, the child will continue to be monitored by the class/subject teachers/tutors.)
5. Review/evaluation:
    SENCO collects information from pupil's reports and requests staff comments, collates the information, discusses with the pupil and parents. Either next IEP is formulated (or it is agreed to remove the pupil from the SEN register).
6. SENCO issues IEP No. 2 and either:
    i) reverts to 5 above as part of a continuous cycle or
    ii) proceeds to 7 and asks for advice from external agencies.
7. Advice in school:
    School asks for advice from external agencies in respect of the nature of the SEN and appropriate resourcing/possible action to be taken as part of School Action. Revert to 5 using information gleaned in continuation of process.

School Action Plus

Identification

As for School Action, the trigger for School Action Plus has regard to the Code of Practice: 'The triggers for School Action Plus could be that, despite receiving an individualised programme and/or concentrated support under School Action, the child:

- Continues to make little or no progress in specific areas over a long period
- Continues working at National Curriculum levels substantially below that expected of children of a similar age
- Continues to have difficulty in developing literacy and mathematics skills
- Has emotional or behavioural difficulties which substantially and regularly interfere with the child's own learning or that of the class or group, despite having an individualised behaviour management programme
- Has sensory or physical needs, and requires additional specialist equipment or regular advice or visits by a specialist service
- Has ongoing communication or interaction difficulties that impede the development of social relationships and cause substantial barriers to learning'

The gathering of information in respect of the pupil's continuing special educational needs may be via:

1. Information gathered from School Action reviews.
2. Liaison with teachers.
3. Liaison with parents.
4. Liaison with outside agencies.

Process for Action, Record-Keeping and Review

1. SENCO gathers information on child from teachers, parents, the child and outside agencies prior to formulating an action plan of support/provision.
2. Individual Education Plan:
   From the collated information, the SENCO discusses the child's needs with the child and the parents and, where appropriate, upon agreement, issues IEP No. 1 at School Action Plus to staff, parents and the child. The support to be provided will be indicated on the IEP. (Where it is deemed there is not enough evidence for the child to be placed at School Action Plus the child will continue at the level of School Action.)
3. Review/evaluation:
   SENCO collects information from pupil's reports and requests staff comments, collates the information, discusses with the pupil and parents. Either next IEP is formulated (or it is agreed to move back to School Action).
4. SENCO reverts to 2 above on a continuous cycle and issues next numbered IEP.

Statutory Assessment/Statement of Special Educational Need

Identification

As outlined in the Code of Practice, 'Where a request for statutory assessment is made by a school to an LEA, the child will have demonstrated significant cause for concern.' The school will provide evidence from:

- The school's action through School Action and School Action Plus.
- Individual education plans for the pupil.
- Records of regular reviews and their outcomes.
- The pupil's health including the child's medical history where relevant.
- National Curriculum levels.
- Attainment in literacy and mathematics.
- Educational and other assessments, for example from an advisory specialist support teacher or an educational psychologist.
- Views of the parents and of the child.
- Involvement of other professionals.
- Any involvement by social services or education welfare service.

Process for Action, Record-Keeping and Review

1. On receipt of a Statement for Special Educational Needs from the local authority, the SENCO will formulate an action plan of support/provision.

2. Individual Education Plan:
   From collated information and advice from external agencies, the SENCO discusses the child's needs with the child and parent and issues IEP No. 1 at Statemented level to staff, parents and child. The support to be provided is indicated and set within short-term targets. (Where the LEA does not issue a statement, the child reverts to School Action Plus.)

3. Review/evaluation:
   Interim Reviews: SENCO collects information from pupil's reports and requests staff comments, collates the information, discusses with the pupil and parents. Either:
   i)   next IEP formulated to continue to next review or
   ii)   annual review initiated early.

4. Annual Review:
   SENCO collects information from staff, parents, child and outside agencies and collates the information prior to the annual review. At the annual review, progress is discussed and either:
   i)   maintain the statement and revert to 2, a continuation of process within school setting
   ii)   request an amendment to the statement
   iii) request ceasing the statement and revert back to School Action Plus.

ACCESS TO THE CURRICULUM

To accommodate pupils who are designated as having a special educational need, the school provides:

- _____ specialist teachers and/or _____ learning support assistants to provide support enabling appropriate access to the curriculum via in-class, small group and individual support.
- Individual teaching programmes designed to meet the needs of each particular child.
- Individualised timetables to accommodate specific needs (this may include disapplication from National Curriculum subjects as agreed through formal requests).
- Specialist equipment.

The school aims to include all pupils with special needs into all the activities of the school as far as it is appropriate. However, in the best interests of the child, there may be occasions or periods of time when the best solution is withdrawal for special intensive programmes to be taught.

Parents and pupils will always be involved in discussion when these situations arise and the pupil's welfare will be the major factor considered when decisions are taken.

Provide a list that gives the names and details of the specialist staff both within school and from outside agencies. Include specialist equipment (not individual items) for example, training equipment to develop fine motor skills. Give details of who has access to it and who has responsibility for it.

EVALUATING SUCCESS

SEN Records

The school SEN records will collate and record the school's responses at all stages and information collected at review meetings will be included. An appropriate combination of the following information regarding individual pupils will be available in school for scrutiny at any time:

Special Needs Register.
Description and nature of pupil's difficulty.
Strategies to be adopted.
Individual Education Plans.
Individual Education Plans evaluation.
Reviews.
Reports from outside agencies.

Monitoring of Provision

The following information is available within school in respect of the effectiveness of the support available for pupils with identified special educational needs. It is gleaned from monitoring and evaluation via observations of:

- Whole class/group teaching.
- Small group/individual teaching.
- In-class support.
- Use of differentiated teaching/resources/specialist equipment.
- Practical use of IEPs.
- Target setting.
- Pupil progress.

Value Added

The notion of 'value added' is an important one to _____School and is monitored by pupil achievements in relation to assessments and results in the following ways:

ii)   examinations/tests, both school based and external
iii)   school's award schemes
iv)   extracurricular activities
v)   work experience success and the destinations at the end of the pupil's school career (*for secondary schools*).

This information provides a valuable insight into the progress of pupils with special educational needs.

The Role of the Governors

The governor with responsibility for SEN will provide termly reports to the whole governing body based on observations and evidence gained from a pre-planned rolling programme of visits.
(*This is heavily dependent on the goodwill of the school's SEN governor and therefore may need altering on number of visits/reports or may even need to be omitted if no such provision is available from the governing body.*)

The whole governing body has a responsibility to produce an annual report which will state the number of students with special educational needs in the school and comment on the school's effectiveness in the implementation of the SEN policy in respect of:
i)   identification of needs
ii)   notification to parents of a child who is deemed to have special educational needs
iii)   assessment of need
iv)   provision for meeting special educational needs

v)   provision of an inclusive environment for all
vi)   methods of monitoring, recording and reporting
vii) SEN funding and spending
viii) deployment of equipment, personnel and resources
ix)   the use made by school of the outside agencies and support services
x)   SEN as an integral part of the school development plan.

PARENT PARTNERSHIP

Contact with Parents

Parents are viewed as partners in their child's education and are kept fully informed about this. They will be contacted directly should there be any change in their child's progress, behaviour or educational provision within school. The process for contact with parents in respect of pupils who have special educational needs will be:

1. SENCO to meet with parents to discuss pupil's placement at School Action and School Action Plus levels.
2. Part of the cycle of reviews to take place at scheduled parents' evenings.
3. SENCO to initiate additional meetings/reviews to take place where appropriate or where there may be a concern over the pupil's progress.
4. SENCO to meet with parents where a request for formal assessment is to be made.
5. In addition to the reviews/parents' evenings, those parents who have a child with a statement of special educational need will be invited to an annual review meeting.

Further to this, the school operates an open-school policy where parents are encouraged to request the opportunity for informal discussion or an organised meeting at any time of their asking. They have the right at any time to access the records relating to their own child and any school documentation they may feel appropriate.

The school will seek to engage the services of a translator where requested by parents or deemed necessary by the SENCO to ensure partnership in developing strategies to help an individual student.

QUERIES AND COMPLAINTS

Parents are partners with the school and are welcome to query decisions made by the school through the school's designated channels as laid down in school documentation. (*Identify which policy in school sets out the procedures for complaints.*)

If on pursuing complaints the parents are not wholly satisfied with the response of the school they may wish to seek further advice/assistance from the LEA. If at this point they do not agree with the school's and LEA's decision, they have a right to appeal to the authority's SEN Tribunal.

IN-SERVICE TRAINING

In-service training is available in respect of SEN for whole school, departmental or individual members of staff. The provision of training will be allocated where there is deemed to be a recognised need and will be in accordance with the school's Professional Development Policy. It will be delivered by one of the following:

- SENCO
- Individual members of staff within the school who have a designated specialism
- LEA support services
- External consultants/trainers

A record of all SEN training delivered and subsequent evaluations will be kept by the SENCO.

EXTERNAL AGENCIES/FACILITIES AND SUPPORT SERVICES

The school works closely with other agencies to focus on the identification and provision for those children who have a special educational need. All services involved with the school are regarded as being part of a working partnership whose aim is to provide, as highlighted in the Code of Practice, an integrated, high quality, holistic support which focuses on the needs of the child.

The following services/agencies are available to/involved with the school:

- Child psychology
- School/pupil support
- Curriculum support
- Sensory and physical impairment
- Emotional and behaviour support
- Home–school tuition
- Education welfare service
- Social services
- Health services
- Child and Adolescent Mental Health Services (CAMHS)
- Connexions Service (*secondary schools*)
- Learning Skills Council (*secondary schools*)
- Voluntary organisations (*list those with whom the school has connections or has input from*)

LINKS WITH OTHER SCHOOLS

Our partner Early Years Providers/Infant Schools/Primary Schools (*choose as appropriate*) are a supportive and welcome contact. Liaison takes place via either the Head, Deputy Head, Assistant Head or the SENCO. (*Choose or add to/remove as appropriate.*) An induction programme for Year _____ pupils coming to_____ School operates in order to establish a welcoming environment.

Liaison with schools in our phase takes place via the Deputy Head/SENCO (*choose or add as appropriate*) who is/are involved in extensive two-way information sharing to ensure adequate information is available regarding any individual pupil and their particular needs.

Links with_____ Special School(s) are established as part of the school's drive towards an inclusive society. This involves:

- shared teaching and learning experiences
- exchange visits as part of the everyday curriculum programme
- shared staff expertise
- shared resources.

Policy last reviewed on ___/___/___ by _____ (*insert name*) SENCO

4 Effective individual education plans

IEPs

Within the government's Green Paper (DfEE 1997) and subsequent booklet *Meeting Special Educational Needs: A Programme of Action* (DfEE 1998), IEPs came under consideration for their effectiveness. In Section 2 (Improving the SEN Framework), the concerns about them were highlighted by the following statement:

> Too often schools focus on the paperwork associated with the Code of Practice – especially in relation to IEPs and annual reviews – at the expense of providing practical support for children with SEN. We want to correct this imbalance. (DfEE 1998: 2:5)

With this in mind, the revised Code of Practice that came into effect in January 2002 (DfES 2001) recommends that an IEP should record the strategies employed to enable the pupil to progress. It further states that, 'The IEP should include information about:

- the short-term targets set for or by the pupil
- the teaching strategies to be used
- the provision to be put in place
- when the plan is to be reviewed
- success and/or exit criteria
- outcomes (to be recorded when the IEP is reviewed)' (DfES 2001: 6:58)

It recommends that 'The IEP should only record that which is additional to or different from the differentiated curriculum provision which is in place as part of provision for all pupils. The IEP should be crisply written and focus on three or four individual targets, chosen from those relating to the key areas of communication, literacy, mathematics and behaviour and social skills to match the pupil's needs. Strategies may be cross-curricular or may sometimes be subject specific. The IEP should be discussed with the pupil and parents' (DfES 2001: 6:59).

In light of the recommendations, let us consider a formula for producing an effective IEP.

The basics of IEPs

What are the essential requirements for producing a good quality IEP that is functional, effective and useful to staff, pupil and parents alike? I would suggest that the following points need to be considered:

- Progress should be charted from recognisable baselines.
- It should contain concise and relevant information about the pupil – think about who needs what information, in what form and for what purpose.
- Available expertise in the school should be used for the skills and strategies that are needed to support the pupil.
- It should form the basis of a partnership between school, pupil, parents and outside agencies (where involved).
- It should map clear roles and responsibilities for all of those involved.
- It must state provision for the child which is different or in addition to general school provision.
- It should be monitored by staff, pupil, parents and outside agencies (where involved) to evaluate the success of learning and progress made.
- Most importantly, it must be both managed and manageable if it is to succeed in its effectiveness.

Taking these points into consideration, let us look at designing an IEP to incorporate the above. From experience I would encourage no more than one side of A4 paper if staff are to access it readily and not feel overwhelmed by the content. Doing this encourages effective use.

A set of criteria I consider a must in the design of an IEP:

1. The nature of the individual's needs.
2. Aims of the IEP.
3. Targets for improvement.
4. Class/subject teacher responsibility (including subject specific if applicable).
5. Support staff responsibility.
6. Pupil responsibility.
7. Help at home.
8. Date for review/evaluation.

These criteria lay the foundations for a positive working document that is able to support the learning of the child. To understand them fully I have taken each one in turn to establish their purpose and value.

1. The nature of the individual's needs

The most important factor in dealing with any individual's special educational needs is the basic understanding of what those needs are. Any teacher who is asked to provide for a pupil's education in a particular, special or differentiated way cannot be expected to do so without understanding what is causing their breakdown in learning.

As a SENCO I would expect to provide a personal profile of the child's needs on the IEP to ensure that the teacher had a constant reminder/aide-memoire. Teachers who take a number of classes per week with a number of pupils in each who have SEN may not readily remember them all in detail.

When producing the profile I would expect to explore a range of information to build up a picture of the child (Fig. 4.1).

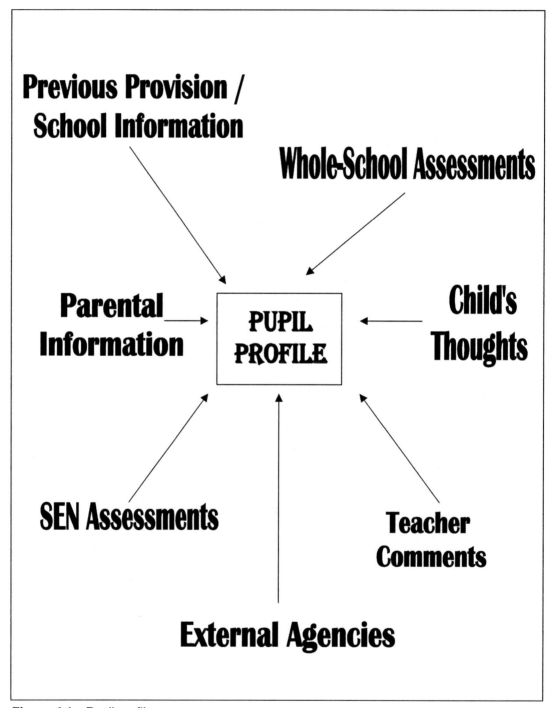

Figure 4.1 Pupil profile

The information gleaned from this can be used to produce a pupil profile. However, it needs to be short, concise and accessible at a glance if it is to be of use to the teacher in the classroom. Also remember, we are working towards one side of A4.

Here is an example of the type and length of profile that may be acceptable:

SAMPLE PROFILE

Reading Age: Accuracy	7.2 – 8.3 (2000)	Spelling Age: 7.1 (2000)
	8.4 – 9.5 (2001)	7.6 (2001)
Comprehension	7.3 – 8.9 (2000)	
	9.2 – 10.1 (2001)	

Dottie has a history of cognitive learning difficulties having problems with both literacy and numeracy skills. Her oral ability and comprehension are better than her reading accuracy and spelling. She does, however, have difficulty on occasions with articulating multisyllabic words. When reading, Dottie makes many errors; she tends to guess at unknown words she doesn't know and substitute visually similar ones. She does not have the skill to segment and sound out unknown words. Her limited knowledge of spelling patterns affects her reading ability. **Do not** ask Dottie to read aloud in class. Dottie has difficulty maintaining concentration and will need help from the teacher to stay on task. She can be difficult to motivate at times; however, she enjoys talking and is able to explain understanding and discuss in detail her perspectives – this should be used by the teacher to encourage Dottie. There is evidence that she has a weak working memory. She cannot recall/recite mathematical tables and will not remember a long series of instructions given orally or alone. Both her mother and previous school state that Dottie can be problematic in lessons and cause disruption in order to avoid the tasks set by the teacher.

Once completed, the profile becomes the basis from which the statement of aims on the IEP is established.

2. Aims of the IEP

The aims of the IEP should inform what the purpose of the document is. This is vital for all concerned but especially for the child. Children need to see what they are being expected to do, from day to day, week to week, but they also need to see and understand how it fits into the 'bigger picture'. They have to be given the opportunity to understand and comprehend the long-term rewards that are to come out of the hard work they are being expected to invest. They will need to feel this investment is worthwhile. Consider, if the IEP is to work for that child, they need to accept the nature of their difficulty, they have to understand how it affects their learning and, most importantly, they need to see a realistic way forward.

On the document itself, all that is required is a short concise statement, for example:

To improve Dottie's literacy and numeracy skills, motivation, self-esteem and provide greater access to the curriculum.

Remember, this needs to be discussed with the child in detail.

With the long-term aims established, the next step is to facilitate a process that will work towards achieving them. How? By setting medium-/short-term targets.

3. Targets for improvement

Targets will establish identified areas for medium-/short-term improvement. They are the stepping-stones towards the skills that will be required to achieve the longer-term aims.

When setting out the targets for improvement, they have to be realistic and achievable. So, where to start? It is a process of building blocks, the foundation of which is the child's profile. This provides the baseline assessment; it tells you where the child is currently and what they can and cannot do. From here targets can be set which will focus on the next set of skills the child needs to acquire.

What happens if you get it wrong? Don't worry, they are not written in tablets of stone. If the pupil is not making sufficient progress and it is apparent that the targets set were not wholly realistic – evaluate, arrange a review, discuss with all involved and set revised targets on a new IEP. If on the other hand the child has achieved the targets – great, but once again, instigate the same process, evaluate, review and set new targets.

Let's return to Dottie at this point and look at a sample set of targets. **Remember**, they must be targets that are achievable in the mainstream classroom and, indeed, beyond.

TARGETS FOR IMPROVEMENT AND SUCCESS/EXIT CRITERIA

i) To develop writing skills by recording information in short sentences/phrases, leading towards extended writing.

ii) To develop reading accuracy skills that allow improvement in access to the curriculum.

iii) To develop listening skills by question/answer techniques to establish more focused concentration.

iv) To improve literacy skills/spelling by focusing on key words to develop a wider vocabulary.

Targets set, now we need to consider ways to implement a programme of action to enable them to be achieved.

When working towards set targets, it is imperative that the responsibility of all involved is established. There is a need to set down actions to be taken that will support the child's learning. With this in mind let us consider what is required from each person.

4. Class/subject teacher responsibility

As you have probably guessed by now, my firm belief is that it is not possible for classroom/subject teachers to deliver individualised programmes of work. (At this point, I have probably become very unpopular in certain quarters!) I would argue that the context in which they are working has to be considered: a class of 30 children, the teacher trying to deliver the curriculum and taking on all of the pressures that this entails. Add to this, pupils who, for a variety of reasons, may need some form of attention or support during the lesson. This does not allow the teacher the luxury to find time to deliver a specified programme of work – unless, of course, they are superhuman! This therefore poses the question – how can classroom/subject teachers support the individual needs of the child? The answer – by adopting support mechanisms, strategies and resources that will cater for the needs of the child.

The following examples give some idea of the range of support mechanisms available (these would not all be on one IEP):

TEACHER RESPONSIBILITY

For the purpose of the example this is written in general terms. When using on an IEP they should be individualised by using the pupil's name.

- Break up instructions into small manageable tasks to ensure the pupil is able to remember them and carry them out.
- To develop the speed of response to instructions and/or tasks, set timed targets for completion which will encourage the pupils to stay on task.
- Where reading is required, group children so that the stronger readers can support the weaker ones.
- When introducing any new vocabulary write it on the board or display it in the classroom. When referring to it, give the pupil the opportunity to repeat it aloud so that they are able to verbalise. Lots of repetition will be needed. Try to use the word in a range of contexts to ensure understanding of meaning has taken place.
- Ask the pupil to write new vocabulary to be learned into their diary/homework book/spelling book.
- Give the pupil plenty of opportunity to express their ideas orally in order to demonstrate their understanding before attempting written work.
- Encourage the use of any of the following: key words, spider charts/mindmaps, flow charts, writing frames, summaries etc., to enable the pupil to organise their written work before attempting to produce extended writing.
- Help the pupil to develop the above strategies into extended pieces of writing.

- Ask the pupil to read through their work on completion, underline any words that they think may be spelt incorrectly and, if they are able, put a circle around the part of the word where they think the mistake is before asking the teacher to mark it.
- When marking the work, mark for content rather than accuracy but do target mark any particular area of weakness that you wish the pupil to focus on.
- If comments are written at the end of a piece of work, make sure they are simple in structure, easy to read and helpful to the pupil in providing understanding of how to develop and improve.
- Ensure the pupil who wears glasses/uses hearing aids/has specialised equipment or resources is making appropriate use of it.

In addition to these, where applicable, I would also encourage an additional section where the subject teachers could set down their own ideas for support in their designated specialist areas.

All of these strategies require no extra staffing and would be appropriate for those pupils identified at the School Action level. For those pupils who are at School Action Plus or have a statement of SEN, you should plan for additional resourcing. This is in line with the Code of Practice's emphasis on a graduated response. It may involve in-class support and/or specialised programmes of work delivered outside of the classroom. This provision would need to be identified on the IEP, including details of named staff who have responsibility.

5. Support staff responsibility

Support staff are generally involved in one of two ways: either in the mainstream classroom or outside the classroom, working with small groups of pupils or individuals. Whichever is the case, the IEP needs to identify their responsibilities. This should involve a statement about the type of provision required and how it is to be carried out. The more detailed information with regard to the support teacher and the targets set should be obtained by daily or weekly planning and recording. An example of such a planning/record sheet (Fig. 4.2) can be found at the end of this chapter. This type of system enables the targets for those pupils at School Action Plus/Statemented to be monitored and adapted constantly.

6. Pupil responsibility

Pupil involvement is imperative. If the child is to achieve the set targets they need to discuss them with the designated teacher responsible. There must be a mutual agreement on what the targets should be and how they are to be achieved. The child, like others involved, must also be given responsibility towards achieving them. Three to four points of responsibility should be specified. For example:

PUPIL RESPONSIBILITY

    i)   Listen carefully to the teacher's instructions and ask for help if I don't understand.

    ii)   Ask for help with my reading from my friends, helper or teacher when I need it.

    iii)   For homework, learn my spellings and what they mean.

    iv)   Read every night with someone at home for 10 minutes.

These four points are all associated with the targets set and they provide the child with responsibilities both in school and at home.

7. Help at home

In respect of those set for home, they now link to the last but not least set of responsibilities – those of the parent/guardian. In order to avoid the problem of outlining whether the child lives with parents, guardians, is in care or has other arrangements I would suggest the title – Help at home. The points outlined here should be closely linked to those of the child, for example, in light of the points made above:

HELP AT HOME

    i)   Listen to _____ read for 10 minutes each evening.

    ii)   Help _____ to learn spellings set by the teacher.

    iii)   Check any homework that has been set and help where necessary.

    iv)   Ask each night how the day has gone. If there are any concerns or worries, contact the school the next morning.

These targets provide for adult support both in learning and in welfare and work towards achieving close links with the school in supporting the learning of the child. They are designed to make the adult feel an important link in the chain of learning, as are all of those involved in the IEP.

Now to the final step of the design, that of review.

8. Date for review/evaluation

This is the smallest item on the IEP but essentially one of the most important. It sets a date for a review of progress leading to evaluation of effectiveness. It provides a focus for achieving set goals within a time limit thus establishing an expectation of improvement.

Who should receive a copy?

Having established the requirements of an IEP and the information contained within, there is finally the question of issuing the finished product. Who should receive a copy?

I would strongly advise that all involved are provided with one, but most definitely those teachers who are involved with the child, irrespective of designation. I am aware that some schools view this as a costly exercise but from experience, where copies are issued to groups or central reference areas, they tend not to become wholly effective working documents.

Sample IEPs

The final part of this chapter is dedicated to what may be the most important part to the reader – sample IEPs. Each takes into account all of the above criteria. They are easy to create on a computer and readily allow progressive updates to be made. This is most definitely a bonus and avoids lengthy rewrites.

It may be that once inspired you wish to create your own. Start from the criteria listed and work with colleagues to look at ways of producing a document that suits your particular circumstances. Have a go – your own designs may well be more successful.

Another consideration are those marketed computerised programmes that are readily available for purchase by schools. Whatever your choice, remember – **it must meet the needs of the child rather than expecting the child to fit its needs!**

Name of Pupil_____ **Date Started**_____

Spelling Progression Checklist

	STAGE 1	To do	Date started	Comments	Date finished
1	Alphabet – visual recognition matching pairs				
2	Letter formation – upper case lower case				
3	Alphabetical order – recite alphabet				
4	Letter sounds – consonants				
5	Common long vowel words				
6	Letter sounds – short vowels a o / i u / e				
7	Sound blending cvc words (onset and rime)				
8	Sentences – capital letters / full stop				
9	Plural with s				
10	Consonant blends – initial position sp st sc sm sl bl cl gl fl pl sn sw tw dr cr gr fr pr br tr				
11	Consonant blends – final position sk st sp lt ct lp xt ld lk lt lf				
12	Consonant digraphs – sh ch th wh				
13	Triple consonant blends – spl spr shr str scr thr				
14	Long vowel, open syllable words				
15	Assimilation – nt nd nch ng nk mp				
16	Suffixing – ed (past tense)				
17	One-syllable words ending in – ll ff ss zz				

continued

		To do	Date started	Comments	Date finished
18	One-syllable words ending in – ck				

19	Vowel consonant digraphs – ar
	                            or
	                            er				

20	'w' rule – wa
	                  – war
	                  – wor				

21	Apostrophe – short forms				
22	'qu' words 'squ' words				
23	– ck plus et / ing / ed				

24	Silent e – long vowels
	Introduce with minimum pairs
	                            a – e
	                            o – e
	                            i – e
	                            u – e
	                            e – e				

25	'v' rule				

26	Soft 'c' says /s/ – initial
	                        medial
	                        final				

27	Soft 'g' says /j/ – initial
	                        medial
	                        final				

28	Words beginning with 'k'				
29	Words beginning with 'j'				
30	'Walls' – qu				
31	– dge				
32	– tch				

33	Long vowel sounds / short vowel spelling
	                        – ind
	                        ild
	                        old
	                        ost				

	End of Stage 1				

Figure 4.2   Spelling progression checklist

SAMPLE INDIVIDUAL EDUCATION PLAN – SCHOOL ACTION

Name:	**Year Group:**	**IEP No. :**
Teacher:	**Class / Department:**	**Date of Issue:**

PUPIL PROFILE – Reading Age: Accuracy –   **Spelling Age:**

Comprehension –

AIMS OF THE IEP

TARGETS FOR IMPROVEMENT

CLASS TEACHER RESPONSIBILITY

SUBJECT SUPPORT

PUPIL RESPONSIBILITY

HELP AT HOME

Date for review of set targets:

Figure 4.3a Sample individual education plan

SAMPLE INDIVIDUAL EDUCATION PLAN – SCHOOL ACTION

Name: Sabina Smiley	**Year Group:** 5	**IEP No. : 1**
Teacher: Mr Magic	**Class / Department:** Group 3 Literacy	**Date of Issue:**

PUPIL PROFILE – Reading Age: Accuracy – 6.9 – 7.10   Spelling Age: 7.3

Comprehension – 6.11 – 8.8

Sabina has some learning difficulties and is currently finding it difficult to cope with life in school. This is affecting her behaviour towards staff and pupils both in and out of the classroom. She does not always understand what to do and gets very distressed if she feels she cannot cope in lessons. Please be patient with Sabina. She finds it very difficult to follow verbal instructions if they are extended and especially if the teacher talks too fast. Her comprehension skills are better than her reading accuracy and spelling. She finds some difficulty in attempting written tasks and may display a number of avoidance strategies when she feels she cannot cope. Please **do not** pressurise Sabina to read aloud in class.

AIMS OF THE IEP

To improve Sabina's understanding and use of both written and verbal language, motivation towards work and behaviour in school.

TARGETS FOR IMPROVEMENT

To develop:
1. i) Sabina's understanding in order to improve her access to the curriculum
2. ii) relationships with both adults and children by improving Sabina's social skills
3. iii) Sabina's writing skills by providing her with structures around which to develop extended writing
4. iv) spelling skills to enhance Sabina's literacy skills

CLASS TEACHER RESPONSIBILITY

To:
1. To give short, step-by-step instructions for Sabina and where possible provide visual cues
2. Provide key words with visual cues for Sabina when introducing new vocabulary
3. Provide writing frames to give structure to Sabina's written work
4. Encourage Sabina to check her work for spelling mistakes and to underline those words she thinks may be incorrect before it is marked
5. Ensure Sabina writes new vocabulary in her spelling book and check for accuracy of the spelling
6. Encourage small-group work with identified members of the class who will provide good role models
7. Encourage Sabina to speak slowly and calmly and give lots of praise when she achieves this
8. Sign Sabina's lesson diary and write a positive sentence when she has done well

SUBJECT SUPPORT

In the Literacy Hour use a lot of visual stimuli to engage the interest of Sabina. Use this to encourage her in the production of written work. Use group work to develop her social skills.

PUPIL RESPONSIBILITY

To: 1.
i 2.   Try to do what I am told and get lots of stickers from the teacher for working hard
i 3.   Check my work for spelling mistakes before I get it marked
i 4.   Ask the teacher to check the spellings in my spelling book
i 5.   Learn my new spellings at home each week
v)   Show my lesson diary at home each night and have it signed

HELP AT HOME

1. Ask to see Sabina's lesson diary each night and sign it. Give lots of praise for lessons where teachers have signed her diary
2. Help Sabina to learn new spellings each week
3. Talk to Sabina about her day at school. Telephone school if there are any concerns and also if there is something she has been really pleased with

Date for review of set targets:

Figure 4.3b   Sample individual education plan

INDIVIDUAL EDUCATION PLAN – SCHOOL ACTION PLUS / STATEMENTED

Name:	**Year Group:**	**IEP No. :**
Teacher:	**Class / Department:**	**Date of Issue:**

PUPIL PROFILE – Reading Age: Accuracy –   **Spelling Age:**

Comprehension –

AIMS OF THE IEP

TARGETS FOR IMPROVEMENT AND SUCCESS / EXIT CRITERIA

CLASS TEACHER RESPONSIBILITY

SUBJECT SUPPORT

SUPPORT STAFF RESPONSIBILITY

PUPIL RESPONSIBILITY

HELP AT HOME

Date for review of set targets:

Figure 4.3c Sample individual education plan

INDIVIDUAL EDUCATION PLAN – SCHOOL ACTION PLUS / STATEMENTED

Name: Henry Happy	Year Group: 8	IEP No. : 3

Teacher: Mr Helpful	Class / Department: History	Date of Issue:

PUPIL PROFILE – Reading Age: Accuracy – 6.10 – 7.11 (Sept 2000)   Spelling Age: 7.3 (Sept 2000)

7.9 – 8.10 (Sept 2001)   7.5 (Sept 2001)

Comprehension – 6.11 – 8.10 (Sept 2000)

7.11 – 9.6 (Sept 2001)

Henry has a history of difficulties in acquiring literacy skills. His self-esteem is low and he is very sensitive about his learning difficulties. He **must** wear glasses for reading and writing. He has some difficulty in articulation, especially saying multisyllabic words. He has a weak short-term memory and cannot recall/recite tables and will not remember a long series of instructions given orally alone. Henry is an inaccurate reader. He misreads words for visually similar ones or guesses them. Please **do not** press him to read aloud in class. He will need help with all reading tasks in lessons. These reading difficulties will compromise his ability to extract meaning from text if he is expected to read alone. Henry's handwriting is irregular and he rarely uses punctuation in written work. His spelling is particularly weak. His oral ability is much better than his written work. Henry is continuing to display behaviour problems both inside and outside the classroom. He gets very frustrated when he is unable to do work set. He has a short concentration span and will need help staying on task and in completing work set.

AIMS OF THE IEP

To improve Henry's literacy skills, motivation and self-esteem, and provide greater access to the curriculum.

TARGETS FOR IMPROVEMENT AND SUCCESS / EXIT CRITERIA

To develop:

    i)   reading skills in order to improve Henry's ability to extract information from text

    ii)   Henry's ability to concentrate by working on timed targets for set tasks

    iii)   Henry's writing skills by providing him with resources, for example, writing frames

    iv)   more self-control by use of identified coping strategies

CLASS TEACHER RESPONSIBILITY

To:

1. Sit Henry by an adequate reader so that when adult support is unavailable he can gain help from a peer
2. Provide differentiated text wherever possible
3. Either class teacher or in-class support staff to set Henry timed targets for completion of tasks
4. Provide the opportunity for Henry to show his better oral ability and reward appropriately
5. Encourage Henry to develop his work through mindmaps to establish his ideas before producing extended written work
6. Provide a range of appropriate writing frames which allow further development of writing from No.4
7. Only correct a **few** targeted spellings at a time. Write the **whole** word for Henry to **see** as you **say** it
8. Give Henry subject specific vocabulary to work on with his support teacher during his specialised programme time
9. Allow Henry to use his 'time-out' card when under pressure from classwork or peers in order to prevent disruption of learning for the class

SUBJECT SUPPORT – Maths

To: Give verbal instructions to Henry particularly where the mathematical work is enveloped in 'wordy' instructions / directions.

SUPPORT STAFF RESPONSIBILITY

Teacher: Mrs Constable to: work on an integrated reading, writing and spelling programme for 2 x 1hour lessons per week.

LSA to: provide support to Henry in class to enable him to achieve his targets and in cooperation with the class teacher, develop resources/strategies to support Henry's learning.

PUPIL RESPONSIBILITY

To:

1. Ask for help from the teacher, Learning Support Assistant or a friend when I cannot get on with my work
2. Put down my ideas by using mindmaps
3. Keep to the times set for my work to be done
4. Learn my spellings given to me by Mrs Constable at home each week
5. Read for 15 minutes every night

HELP AT HOME

1. Help Henry to learn his spellings each week
2. Read together with Henry every night
3. Check that he understands his homework
4. Talk to Henry about his day at school. Telephone school if there are any concerns and also if there is something he has been really pleased with

Date for review of set targets:

Figure 4.3d   Sample individual education plan

5 Reviewing progress

The review process

The process is one of several strands of action being pulled together enabling a full evaluation of the pupil's progress. This evaluation must be in relation to set targets outlined on the IEP. The process should culminate in a review meeting that provides the opportunity for informed discussion and results in future action to be taken. The meeting needs careful consideration and organisation if it is to be both successful and useful.

When should the reviews take place?

For SENCOs, this is often a major issue. If a school has a considerable number of pupils with SEN, it can be a nightmare to fit them all in! It definitely requires good strategic planning.

I would suggest that putting review dates for pupils with SEN on the school's yearly calendar is a must. Through discussion and prior planning in relation to whole-school arrangements, and in conjunction with the SENCO's calendar, a spread of workload across the academic year should be possible.

In the Code of Practice, the advice in respect of the IEP review states:

• Reviews should be at least twice a year
• At least one review could coincide with a routine parent's evening
• They need not be unduly formal
• Parents' views should be sought
• The child should take part in the review process

Taking these points into consideration, it would seem that when deciding on dates for reviews, at least one could be in line with already planned parents' evenings. These are the ones that are decided upon by the school's management team and placed on the whole-school calendar prior to the start of each year. I would also suggest, wherever possible, the timings of annual reports should be taken into consideration when making a decision on a time for a review. Think of streamlining the paperwork!

Careful thought should also be given to the responsibility and pressure placed on the SENCO – is he/she the only person who can carry out a review? The answer is most definitely no! Other teachers are certainly capable of taking part in the process and appropriately organised delegation should be considered by all schools for at least one of the reviews.

Let us look at the organisation of a review system that takes into account minimal paperwork/maximum information.

Pre-meeting

The action prior to the meeting involves both information sharing and information gathering. Parents, teachers and outside agencies must be informed of the date of the meeting well in advance and at the same time, requests can be made for comments/reports on the progress of the pupil. All information will need to be gathered, collated and sent out to all parties involved prior to the actual meeting. At this stage of the process, the SENCO's workload can be alleviated greatly as this work can most certainly be done by an effective administrative assistant. For example, they could carry out the following:

- Six weeks before the review date send out invitations to meeting and requests for information.
- Four weeks prior to meeting chase up any replies and requests for information not received.
- Two weeks before the meeting collate the gathered information and provide a copy to the SENCO for approval.
- One week before the meeting send out the collated information to all parties attending the meeting.

To facilitate the above, a simple standardised set of letters and proformas held on computer file will make the administrator's job a relatively easy task and will most certainly reduce the input required by the SENCO.

Gathering the information

The information gathering part of the exercise should aim to be as painless as possible.

Within school
Being mindful of the concerns relating to the reduction in bureaucracy as highlighted in the publication *Meeting Special Educational Needs: A Programme of Action* (DfEE 1998), this needs careful thought.

The request for and collection of evidence/information will depend on what is readily at hand. Is there a computerised system that provides for all of the requirements? If the answer is yes, brilliant – but if this is not the case it unfortunately has to be a paper exercise. At this point, think about ready established recording and reporting systems already in place and consider how they can be utilised. Is there a need to issue specific paperwork? If this is the case, careful thought must be given to its content. I would suggest that the paperwork should be relatively easy to complete and definitely **not** time-consuming if it is to be effective. Where on collection of evidence there is cause for concern, the SENCO may request more detailed information but where sufficient progress is evident, there is less of a need to gather together extensive proof of progression and a précis will surely suffice.

External agencies

In the case of the external agencies, it would be expected that they will produce a standardised report from their own service. There may be occasions, however, when the school may request specific items of information that are pertinent to a particular review. These should be stated in the letter of invitation, alerting the service of the need to include those particular items within their report.

Parents

Where parents are concerned, it may be that a simple comment form could be issued which requests information about their view of their child's progress both in school and at home. Be mindful – some parents may have similar difficulties to their children and find this a daunting task.

Children

It would be helpful if the school could provide a simple comment form for the child to complete, either at home with the parent or in school with a trusted adult. The intention of the form is to ascertain the child's view of their progress. This process must be non-threatening if the child's feelings and thoughts are to be of value.

Information sharing

Once collected, the administrative assistant may produce a pack of information that the SENCO is able to read through and approve prior to being sent out to all parties attending the review. At this stage of the process, a screening of progress can take place and an informed decision made as to who is to carry out the review. Those pupils who give no cause for concern may be reviewed by a designated teacher while those giving cause for concern may be reviewed by the SENCO. This system works on the basis of those children whose needs are being met, and who are progressing well, requiring less formalised reviews than those who are not.

The review meeting

Organisation

The organisation of the meetings will be very dependent on the child's individual needs. As already suggested, where sufficient progress is being made, one of the reviews may take place with a class teacher or a form tutor during set organised parents' evenings. If there is concern over a child, the SENCO may meet with the parents of the child during the same evening.

The second review should be organised at set times during the year that ensure a sufficient period of time between the two reviews for them to be of value. This review may involve support staff and/or the SENCO, once again the person(s) involved being dependent on the pupil's progress.

Points for consideration

Irrespective of the nature of the meeting – whether it is a parents' evening or a specifically arranged time, and whether it is carried out by a designated teacher or the SENCO – the following points must be covered:

- consideration of all gathered information
- discussion and evaluation of progress made in relation to set targets and overall progress including effectiveness of support mechanisms in place
- setting of future targets and future support
- setting the date of the next review.

At both meetings, the parents and the child should be consulted and new targets set. If this creates a difficulty for either party, the parents may be contacted by telephone while the target-setting part of the process could be incorporated into the SENCO/SEN department's daily work within the school.

Keeping a record

Most of the above points are considered at a parents' evenings for all pupils, so there is very little extra effort required by those involved. It will, however, require a certain amount of paperwork in order to record the outcomes of the meeting. This is of value to the school as a whole, not just for pupils with SEN, as it is a way of providing evidence of progression and involves action to be taken where required.

Where pupils with SEN are concerned, the outcome of the process must result in a complete record in the pupil's SEN file that is able to comment on the effectiveness of the provision and progress made, future targets for improvement, the nature of the support to be allocated and the date of the next review.

Are two reviews a year enough?

In most circumstances, two reviews a year are enough, however, there will be those children who, at some time in their school career, may not be progressing adequately and therefore may need a further review in addition to those already planned. This review is most certainly down to the SENCO. These are the children who will need to be monitored closely over shorter periods of time with appropriate action being taken. Pupils who have a statement of SEN **must**, by law, have an annual review; once again this should be the SENCO's responsibility. These reviews should take place at times during the year that are pertinent to particular year groups and are in addition to the IEP reviews. As suggested in the Code, dates chosen for the review should 'reflect the circumstances of the child and the action that may follow from the review, for example, a move to a secondary school'.

The annual review for pupils with a statement of SEN

The Code of Practice sets out in its introduction to the Annual Review (DfES 2001: 9:1) that a statement review ensures:

- Pupil progress over a 12 month period is monitored by the school, parents, all professionals involved and the LEA.
- Amendments required (if any) to the description of need are considered.
- Amendments required (if any) to provision are considered.
- Monitoring of provision.
- Evaluation of provision.

The Code also points out that in particular circumstances,

i) Interim reviews may be arranged for those pupils that a school may identify as being at serious risk of disaffection or exclusion.

ii) The annual review in Year 9 involves a transitional plan and should therefore involve the agencies that play a major role in the young person's post-school years. It **must** involve the Connexions Service. (Connexions is the service that is available to all 14–19-year-olds. It provides support and guidance in respect of the pupil's transition towards work and adulthood. It is a vital service for those pupils with SEN.)

In order to **ensure**, LEAs and schools should have in place a system that facilitates the following points:

- The LEA **must** write to all head teachers no less than two weeks before the start of each term with a list of pupils on roll at their school who will require an annual review that term.
- The head teacher or designated person **must** provide the LEA with a report following each annual review meeting before the end of that term, or ten school days after the meeting takes place if that is any earlier.

- The head teacher or designated person **must** request written advice from the child's parents, anyone specified by the authority and anyone else considered appropriate.
- The head teacher or designated person **must** circulate a copy of all advice received to all of those invited to the review meeting at least two weeks before the date of the meeting, inviting additional comments, including comments of those unable to attend the meeting.
- The head teacher or designated person **must** invite to the review meeting the child's parents (guardian), a relevant teacher (more often than not the SENCO), a representative whom the LEA deems appropriate and any other person considered appropriate.

Where the school is involved, the work can be achieved by the SENCO and administrative assistant while working within the guidelines set down by the LEA. I would suggest the system could be aligned to that already established for IEP reviews, avoiding the creation of extra work.

What about the paperwork?

As stated earlier in this chapter, the paperwork needs to be as streamlined and painless as possible. Careful thought needs to be given as to how much information is required and in what format. Ask the question – what exactly do I need to know and for what purpose?

The following proformas provide a package of paperwork for the review process. Taking all of the points raised in this chapter into account, the intention is to demonstrate an example of a workable system. This is not a definitive package but rather intended to give help/support to schools/colleagues.

<table>
<tr><td colspan="6" align="center">__SEN Pupil Information__</td></tr>
<tr><td colspan="2">__SA–School Action__</td><td colspan="2">__SAP–School Action Plus__</td><td colspan="2">__ST–Statemented__</td></tr>
</table>

Year Group _____   Subject (if applicable)_____

The following sheet gives pupil and their level of SEN. Please complete their NC Level and tick the appropriate box to indicate whether the pupil is progressing (PM – progress made) or giving cause for concern (CfC). Where there is an indication of a pupil giving cause for concern could you please enter in the notes section a brief précis of your concerns, i.e. inadequate reading / writing skills, inability to access information, poor concentration, lack of understanding, poor behaviour.

Name	SA / SAP ST	NC Level	PM	CfC	Notes

Many thanks for your cooperation and support.

_____ (SENCO)

Figure 5.1a SEN pupil information

SEN Pupil Information

SA–School Action **SAP–School Action Plus** **ST–Statemented**

Year Group _____   Subject (if applicable)_____

The following sheet gives pupil and their level of SEN. Please complete their NC Level and tick the appropriate box to indicate whether the pupil is progressing (PM – progress made) or giving cause for concern (CfC). Where there is an indication of a pupil giving cause for concern could you please enter in the notes section a brief précis of your concerns, i.e. inadequate reading / writing skills, inability to access information, poor concentration, lack of understanding, poor behaviour.

Name	SA / SAP ST	NC Level	PM	CfC	Notes
Alan Arbuckle	ST				
Brenda Bonce	SA				
Fiona Ferris	SA				
Harpreet Hussain	SAP				
Jason Juniper	SAP				
Nerris Noon	SA				
Rhianne Roley	SAP				
Simon Swan	SA				
Vijay Patel	SA				
Theresa Triangle	SA				
William Waterhouse	SA				

Many thanks for your cooperation and support.

_____ (SENCO)

Figure 5.1b SEN pupil information

SEN Pupil Information

SA–School Action   **SAP–School Action Plus**   **ST–Statemented**

Year Group _____   Subject (if applicable)_____

The following sheet gives pupil and their level of SEN. Please complete their NC Level and tick the appropriate box to indicate whether the pupil is progressing (PM – progress made) or giving cause for concern (CfC). Where there is an indication of a pupil giving cause for concern could you please enter in the notes section a brief précis of your concerns, i.e. inadequate reading / writing skills, inability to access information, poor concentration, lack of understanding, poor behaviour.

Name	SA / SAP ST	NC Level	PM	CfC	Notes
Alan Arbuckle	ST	2		/	Poor understanding, reading, writing. Not coping at all.
Brenda Bonce	SA	3	/		
Fiona Ferris	SA	3	/		
Harpreet Hussain	SAP	4	/		
Jason Juniper	SAP	2		/	Poor behaviour stops any work so difficult to assess ability/ progress.
Nerris Noon	SA	3	/		
Rhianne Roley	SAP	5	/		
Simon Swan	SA	3	/		
Vijay Patel	SA	2		/	Reads well, accesses information well but writing extremely poor.
Theresa Triangle	SA	3	/		
William Waterhouse	SA	2		/	Very concerned with all literacy and numeracy skills. Needs more help.

Many thanks for your cooperation and support.

_____ (SENCO)

Figure 5.1c SEN pupil information

SEN Record of Progress – KS1 & KS2

Name: _____ D.O.B. _____

School Action ☐   School Action Plus ☐   Statemented ☐

Nature of Difficulty: Cognitive ☐   Communication ☐   EBD ☐

Physical/Sensory ☐   Medical ☐

	Yr.1	Yr.2	Yr.3	Yr.4	Yr.5	Yr.6
Reading Age						
Spelling Age						
Other						
_____						
_____						

Review No.:	1　2	1　2	1　2	1　2	1　2	1　2
NC levels						
Eng/Lit						
Maths/Num						
Science						
History						
Geography						
D & T						
Art						
Music						
PE						
RE						
ICT						

Figure 5.2a   SEN record of progress at Key Stages 1, 2, 3 and 4

	SEN Record of Progress – KS3 & KS4

Name: _____ D.O.B. _____

School Action ☐ School Action Plus ☐ Statemented ☐

Nature of Difficulty: Cognitive ☐ Communication ☐ EBD ☐

Physical/Sensory ☐ Medical ☐

	Yr.1	Yr.2	Yr.3	Yr.4	Yr.5	Yr.6
Reading Age						
Spelling Age						
Other						
_____						
_____						
Review No.:	1 2 NC Levels	1 2 NC Levels	1 2 NC Levels	1 2 NC Levels	1 2 NC Levels	1 2 NC Levels
Eng/Lit						
Maths/Num						
Science						
M.F.L.						
History						
Geography						
D & T						
Art						
Music						
PE						
RE						
ICT						
Citizenship						

Figure 5.2b SEN record of progress at Key Stages 1, 2, 3 and 4

Pupil Comment Sheet

Try to answer the following questions to the best of your ability.

Name : ______________________________ Signature: __________________

Do you think that you are doing well with your school work?

What do you like best about school?

What worries you most about school?

What do you find hard to do at home?

Is there anything you can think of that would help you more at school or at home?

Figure 5.3 Pupil comment sheet

ISBN 1 85346 802 9, published by David Fulton Publishers

Parent / Guardian Comment Sheet

Please could you complete the following information and return it to school before the review date which is given in the letter you have received with this sheet.

Name of your child: ______________________________

Name of parent / guardian: ____________________________ Signature: __________________

Do you think your son / daughter is happy at school?

Are you satisfied with the progress he / she is making?

Are you happy with your son / daughter at home?

Further comments you may wish to make (continue over the page if needed)

Figure 5.4 Parent/guardian comment sheet

ISBN 1 85346 802 9, published by David Fulton Publishers

Review Meeting Record

Name: _____ Class: _____ Date of Meeting: _____

Member of Staff i/c _____ Designation _____

Involved in meeting / Comments attached:

Parent / Guardian ☐ Pupil ☐ Other ☐ Please state:_____
                                                        _____
Comments attached ☐ ☐ ☐   _____

Progress: *enter main points discussed at the meeting with regard to pupil progress.*

Action to be taken: *list points of action to be initiated.*

Targets set:

Next review date:

Figure 5.5 Review meeting record

6 Support for learning – school – teacher – pupil

Consider this.

When organising support for learning in schools there are a number of factors that need to be taken into consideration. How do we decide on who is to get support? How and when is it to be provided? Who is involved? How can a whole programme of support be organised? Who gains from the support? Is it cost effective and good value for money?

These are just some of the questions that need to be answered. The starting point I suggest is the Code of Practice and its emphasis on a graduated response. If this is to be achieved, consideration needs to be given to the whole school, the classroom teacher and the pupil in turn. With good planning and organisation, the three areas when pulled together can form a network of support which, if organised well, will provide an efficient and an effective service for meeting the needs of the children. The support mechanisms in school are the crux for effective provision for pupils with SEN. Irrespective of how well IEPs are written, information is shared with staff and guidelines given, if access to learning is not facilitated the rest becomes meaningless.

School support

There is good reason for starting with the whole school. If children are to access learning and achieve to the best of their ability, schools must look carefully at the curriculum they offer. By good planning, organisation and evaluation, a school may design a curriculum to meet the majority of the needs of the children in its care. This also allows schools to minimise the number of pupils requiring more specific support and therefore to be able to target those in need more effectively.

With a whole-school view of a pupil's accessibility to learning, the SENCO ought to be regarded as an invaluable source of information and expertise when it comes to planning the curriculum. Their involvement should be at a managerial level but, even if this is not the case, they should at the very least be asked for information and advice on a range of matters. Figure 6.1 outlines the areas in which a positive contribution could be made.

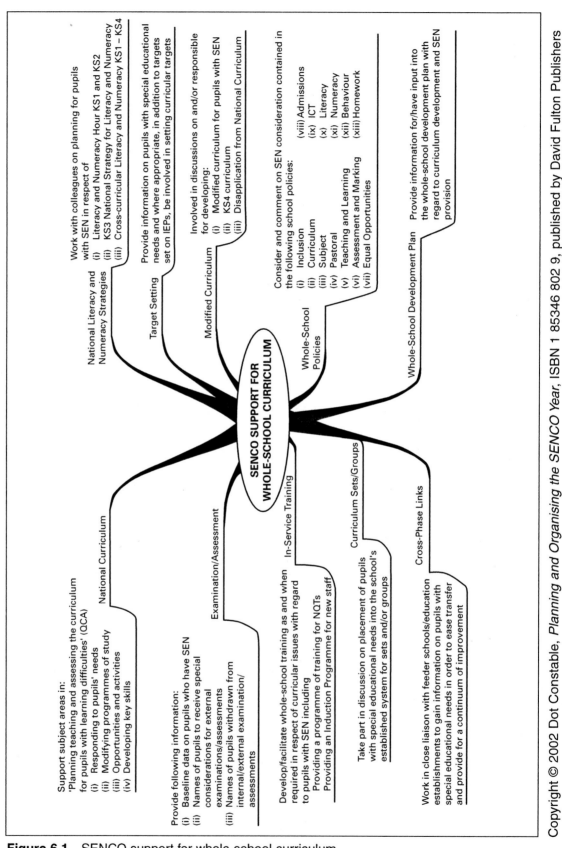

Figure 6.1 SENCO support for whole-school curriculum

The diagram does not provide a definitive list and there may be other areas that need consideration. I would say, however, that the amount of time individual schools allocate to the SENCO may well influence their involvement. It may also depend on the status of the SENCO within the school as to how their input is regarded and what effect it has on decisions made. As the Code of Practice points out, 'Many schools find it effective for the SENCO to be a member of the senior leadership team' (DfES 2001: 5:34, 6:37) – this should be considered by all schools!

Classroom teacher support

Once the curriculum is established, the next step is to ascertain how teachers are to facilitate learning for those pupils who are unable to access it fully without some form of support. These are the pupils who will be designated as having SEN.

With some pupils, teaching techniques, adapted resources and delivery styles will suffice. For others there may be a need for in-class support or small-group teaching. Whatever the provision, SENCOs need to provide support/training for teachers to ensure the following points are considered, understood and acted upon.

Types of learning difficulties

The Code of Practice identifies the following areas for consideration:

- Cognition and learning difficulties.
- Emotional or behavioural difficulties.
- Sensory or physical needs.
- Communication or interaction difficulties.
- Medical problems.

Teachers must be aware of the needs of the children in their care and therefore it would be expected that the SENCO would provide general information/training to all staff on these. It is essential that schools provide staff with a broad-based general knowledge of types of need – not just for catering for those needs but also, just as importantly, in order to recognise them. More specific, in-depth knowledge/information may then be provided for the classroom teacher(s) involved with identified pupils, thus building on the foundation of basic understanding. This may be achieved via IEPs, pupil profiles, information sheets or meetings with staff.

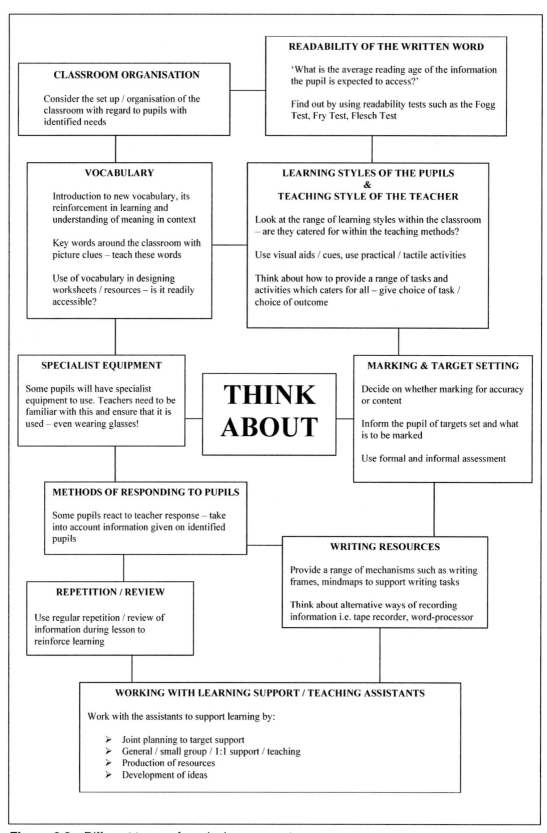

CLASSROOM ORGANISATION

Consider the set up / organisation of the classroom with regard to pupils with identified needs

READABILITY OF THE WRITTEN WORD

'What is the average reading age of the information the pupil is expected to access?'

Find out by using readability tests such as the Fogg Test, Fry Test, Flesch Test

VOCABULARY

Introduction to new vocabulary, its reinforcement in learning and understanding of meaning in context

Key words around the classroom with picture clues – teach these words

Use of vocabulary in designing worksheets / resources – is it readily accessible?

LEARNING STYLES OF THE PUPILS
&
TEACHING STYLE OF THE TEACHER

Look at the range of learning styles within the classroom – are they catered for within the teaching methods?

Use visual aids / cues, use practical / tactile activities

Think about how to provide a range of tasks and activities which caters for all – give choice of task / choice of outcome

SPECIALIST EQUIPMENT

Some pupils will have specialist equipment to use. Teachers need to be familiar with this and ensure that it is used – even wearing glasses!

THINK ABOUT

MARKING & TARGET SETTING

Decide on whether marking for accuracy or content

Inform the pupil of targets set and what is to be marked

Use formal and informal assessment

METHODS OF RESPONDING TO PUPILS

Some pupils react to teacher response – take into account information given on identified pupils

WRITING RESOURCES

Provide a range of mechanisms such as writing frames, mindmaps to support writing tasks

Think about alternative ways of recording information i.e. tape recorder, word-processor

REPETITION / REVIEW

Use regular repetition / review of information during lesson to reinforce learning

WORKING WITH LEARNING SUPPORT / TEACHING ASSISTANTS

Work with the assistants to support learning by:

➢ Joint planning to target support
➢ General / small group / 1:1 support / teaching
➢ Production of resources
➢ Development of ideas

Figure 6.2 Different types of curriculum support

Copyright © 2002 Dot Constable, *Planning and Organising the SENCO Year*, ISBN 1 85346 802 9, published by David Fulton Publishers

Information on appropriate types of support for designated needs

Once understanding of need is established, teachers will require ideas, strategies, and information on how best to support those needs in the mainstream classroom. There are a wealth of support mechanisms too numerous to mention but they can be categorised into type (see Fig. 6.2) and issued to colleagues with examples/thoughts to be considered. Where further information is required, the SENCO/SEN support staff may be involved in working with individuals or groups of teachers on specific programmes of work developing a range of ideas, strategies and plans to facilitate the learning of identified pupils. By providing staff with mechanisms for support one can then have an expectation of informed planning.

Use of IEPs and pupil information to inform planning of lessons

With prior knowledge of a pupil, understanding of the difficulties encountered when accessing the curriculum and a range of support mechanisms available, the classroom teacher is now well equipped to make informed judgements on how to cater for the individual's needs. At the start of each academic year, this may cause some stress on planning due to the number of children to be catered for, however, once staff become familiar with the children, it will become more of an automatic part of their short-, medium- and long-term planning. Where planning is concerned, it may result in changes to the curriculum, its content and delivery as teachers often find that when searching for solutions to one child's difficulties it results in better access for all.

The SENCO's input to teacher support

When planning for teacher support, the SENCO may provide some by facilitating whole-school training, some by departmental training and some by working with individual teachers who need specific support. Consideration should be taken of the expertise of colleagues both in school and beyond when organising the support. Sharing ideas, resources and strategies is essential. The old adage stands firm – 'Why reinvent the wheel?' Most important is that, whatever the methodology, the outcome must be the same: facilitating SEN provision that enables the pupil(s) to learn effectively.

Pupil support

Following on from teacher support, with an emphasis on a graduated response, where the needs of the child are unable to be met by appropriate curriculum, teaching and resourcing, further input will be required. The support allocated for such pupils will require adult/peer intervention in any one or a number of the following areas:

- Reading.
- Writing.
- Listening.
- Understanding.
- Communication.
- Numeracy/mathematical skills.
- Social skills/behaviour.
- Development of self-esteem.
- Production of work in a range of subject areas.

Where peer support is appropriate, the directives should be laid out on the pupil's IEP for the attention of the class teacher. Where adult support is required, the intervention planned will vary according to need and may be via in-class, small group or individual support. Whatever the allocation, there is a definite requirement on the part of the SENCO to organise and formulate a planned response. This is to ensure that where in-class support takes place there is no duplication of personnel – I have observed lessons where in addition to the teacher there were three other adults present in the lesson. It also enables good planning in response to a pupil's withdrawal from mainstream lessons – missing the same lesson all year is not a good idea.

With both of these issues in mind, support needs to be organised in a logical and time efficient manner. For colleagues in large secondary schools this can be a daunting task. From experience, I found developing methods of allocation and timing of support sessions best done on a computerised system. By using a colour-coded system for identifying staff and working on a school timetable plan, it was much easier to see where clashes took place and where staff had been allocated to two different lessons during the same period. Once completed, it was relatively easy to take note of where individual pupils were receiving support and from whom. If a computerised system is unavailable then unfortunately it has to become a paper exercise. However, the same methods can be used by placing the timetable on a board and using coloured pins.

Once the system for support is in place and the provision for individual pupils is decided upon, as a SENCO I would wish to have in place a set of guidelines on 'support for learning'. It would be beneficial if some form of in-service training were provided to all staff initially to enhance their awareness (this should be repeated at least annually to take into account new staff). The focus of the training should be to provide understanding of the need for strong working partnerships and the ways in which they may be developed. Having delivered the training, the guidelines may be used as an aide-mémoire. The advice given should not be so prescriptive as to prevent staff working to their strengths, but should at least set out the possible types of provision and a set of expectations to be met by both SEN staff and mainstream teachers. The simple guidance sheet at the end of this chapter (Fig. 6.5) provides an example of the type of information that may be given.

The final hurdle on organisation of support is the record-keeping for both support staff and teachers. It is vital if the SENCO is to be kept informed on pupil progress and suitability of provision and to be able to evaluate its overall effectiveness. The system of paperwork for this purpose needs to be simple and straightforward and must not overly impose on the time spent working with the pupils. Taking this into consideration, I would suggest that records by mainstream teachers should include a coding system to be used on their own planning sheets/pupil registers/records (see Fig. 6.3). At the same time, support staff may complete a brief lesson record and use the same codes to define their own input (see Fig. 6.4). This record sheet will suffice irrespective of in-class or withdrawal support sessions thus ensuring the system remains simplistic and streamlined.

Questions answered

At the beginning of this chapter a set of questions was raised in relation to support for learning. It is hoped that by the information which followed they have, in some way, been answered. There are no hard and fast rules for schools to follow when organising their own support systems, but they should be geared to the needs of the pupils in their care. They should ultimately work towards developing independent learners who have formulated their own sets of strategies and systems to overcome their difficulties and who are able to continue along the path of lifelong learning. If schools achieve this, they will have surely succeeded.

<u>Codes for Lesson Records</u>

One-to-one work	**1:1**
Small-group work	**SGW**
General in-class support	**GIS**
Withdrawal from mainstream lessons	**WML**
Resources – production/adaptation of	**RES**

For the classroom teacher, the codes may be used in one of the two following ways:

At the heading stage of a lesson record sheet to demonstrate the type of support to be given –

Lesson Planning Record

Lesson: _____ Subject:_____ Date: _____

Teacher: _____ Support teacher / assistant: _____

Type of support: 1:1 ☐ SGW ☐ GIS ☐ WML ☐ RES ☐

No. of pupils with SEN:

School Action ☐ School Action Plus ☐ Statemented ☐

On the class register where there is a need to signify where children are being taught outside of the mainstream classroom –

Class Register

SA – School Action   SAP – School Action Plus   ST – Statemented

Name	SEN	13/9	20/9	27/9	4/10	11/10	18/10	1/11	8/11	15/11
M. Abrahams	SAP	/	WML	0	WML	/	WML			
D. Alexander		/	/	0	/	/	/			
S. Callendar	SA	/	/	/	/	/	/			
H. Delaney		/	/	/	/	/	0			
G. Farooq		0	/	/	/	/	/			
M. Kaur	ST	WML	/	WML	0	WML	/			
R. Marley		0	/	/	/	/	/			

Figure 6.3 Codes for lesson records

<u>Support for Learning - Lesson Record Sheet</u>

Date: **Class:** **Subject:**

Teacher: **Support Teacher / Assistant:**

Type of support – 1:1 ☐ SGW ☐ GIS ☐ WML ☐ RES ☐
(You may need to tick more than one box)

Lesson Content / Objectives

Pupil(s) Supported:

Notes:

Figure 6.4 Support for learning – lesson record sheet

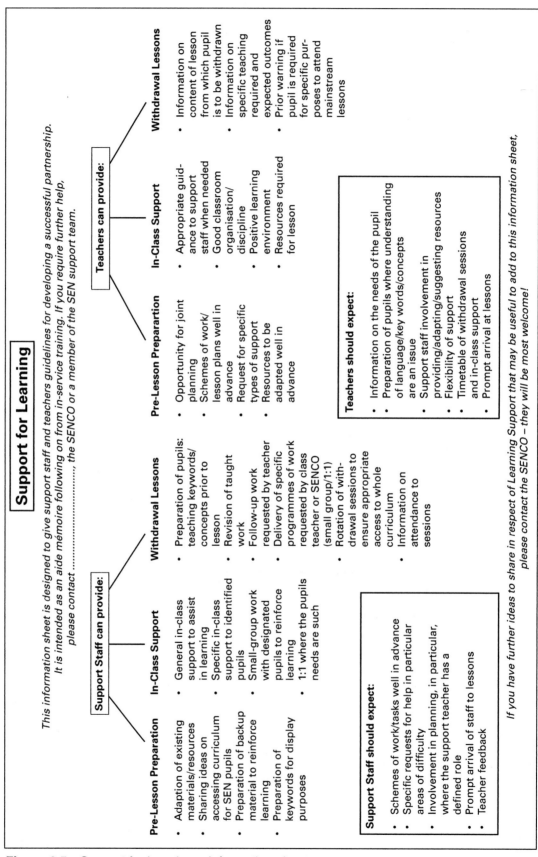

Support for Learning

This information sheet is designed to give support staff and teachers guidelines for developing a successful partnership. It is intended as an aide mémoire following on from in-service training. If you require further help, please contact ...., the SENCO or a member of the SEN support team.

Support Staff can provide:

Pre-Lesson Preparation
- Adaption of existing materials/resources
- Sharing ideas on accessing curriculum for SEN pupils
- Preparation of backup material to reinforce learning
- Preparation of keywords for display purposes

In-Class Support
- General in-class support to assist in learning
- Specific in-class support to identified pupils
- Small-group work with designated pupils to reinforce learning
- 1:1 where the pupils needs are such

Withdrawal Lessons
- Preparation of pupils: teaching keywords/concepts prior to lesson
- Revision of taught work
- Follow-up work requested by teacher
- Delivery of specific programmes of work requested by class teacher or SENCO (small group/1:1)
- Rotation of withdrawal sessions to ensure appropriate access to whole curriculum
- Information on attendance to sessions

Support Staff should expect:
- Schemes of work/tasks well in advance
- Specific requests for help in particular areas of difficulty
- Involvement in planning, in particular, where the support teacher has a defined role
- Prompt arrival of staff to lessons
- Teacher feedback

Teachers can provide:

Pre-Lesson Preparation
- Opportunity for joint planning
- Schemes of work/lesson plans well in advance
- Request for specific types of support
- Resources to be adapted well in advance

In-Class Support
- Appropriate guidance to support staff when needed
- Good classroom organisation/discipline
- Positive learning environment
- Resources required for lesson

Withdrawal Lessons
- Information on content of lesson from which pupil is to be withdrawn
- Information on specific teaching required and expected outcomes
- Prior warning if pupil is required for specific purposes to attend mainstream lessons

Teachers should expect:
- Information on the needs of the pupil
- Preparation of pupils where understanding of language/key words/concepts are an issue
- Support staff involvement in providing/adapting/suggesting resources
- Flexibility of support
- Timetable of withdrawal sessions and in-class support
- Prompt arrival at lessons

If you have further ideas to share in respect of Learning Support that may be useful to add to this information sheet, please contact the SENCO – they will be most welcome!

Figure 6.5   Support for learning – information sheet

7 Collaborative working

Who is involved?

There are a number of groups who are required to work with a school in order to provide a wider network of support for those pupils with SEN. In the previous chapter, the importance of the working relationship between teachers and support staff was emphasised. This is equally important when the network widens and parents, external agencies and the LEA become involved.

The Code of Practice highlights the need for collaborative working with parents,

> Partnership with parents plays a key role in promoting a culture of co-operation between parents, schools, LEAs and others. This is important in enabling children and young people with SEN to achieve their potential. (DfES 2001: 2:1)

and with external agencies,

> Many children and young people with SEN have a range of difficulties and the achievement of educational objectives is likely to be delayed without partnership in the pupil's education between all concerned. Thus support for pupils with special needs requires a concerted approach from health professionals, social services departments (SSD), specialist LEA support services and other providers of support services including the Connexions Service. All these services should aim to provide an integrated service for the child so that the parents and the pupil perceive the provision as 'seamless'. (DfES 2001: 6:29)

If this type of sound collaborative system is to be established it may need to be facilitated by the school which the pupil attends. If this is the case, it is most likely to be the SENCO who takes responsibility for establishing this working relationship. For this to be achieved, there are a certain number of requirements that need to be met and they should be based on the principle of the greater the need, the wider the network of support and collaboration required. The starting point is the school's working relationship with the parent(s) for without this, widening support becomes more difficult to achieve.

Working with parents

Schools have in place home/school agreements which should be the starting point for establishing a working relationship with the parent. Statements of expectation contained in this document can indicate the school's commitment to the parent and the child in respect of SEN. At the same time, it can also set out an expectation to the parent of what in turn the school expects of them, for example:

As a school we will try to:

- Care for your child's safety and happiness within the school and provide them with a safe environment in which to learn.
- Ensure your child achieves their full potential taking into account the whole-school experience of your child.
- Provide a balanced curriculum and meet the individual needs of your child.
- Achieve high standards of work and behaviour by building good relationships and a sense of responsibility.
- Keep you informed about school matters and, in particular, about the progress of your child.
- Be open and welcoming at all times and offer you the opportunities to be involved in the life of the school.

As guardian(s) we/I shall try to ensure that:

- Our/my child arrives at school on time and attends regularly.
- Our/my child is properly equipped for all lessons.
- We/I will contact the school with any concerns with regard to work/behaviour/happiness.
- We/I will support the school's policies and guidelines for behaviour.
- We/I will support our/my child's learning at home.
- We/I will support parents' evenings and meetings to discuss the progress of our/my child.
- We/I will endeavour to get to know the school and support it in all that it does to provide a quality whole-school educational experience for our/my child.

With these kinds of statements in place, the SENCO may feel confident about contacting parents in respect of their child's SEN. It is worth bearing in mind at this point that whenever parents are involved with the school, both have rights of access to information and discussion even if a separation has taken place between them.

The method of contact will depend on how easily accessible the parent is. In Key Stages 1 and 2 for example, parents are often in contact with the school and it would be more appropriate to arrange a meeting by word of mouth. Where this is not possible, and in respect of secondary schools where parents do not as a rule take their children to school, I would suggest contact by telephone. In both cases, word of mouth should be regarded as most important particularly if the SENCO is notifying the parent for the first time that their child may have a learning difficulty. The personal approach has several benefits:

- Parents of the child have immediate opportunity to ask questions.
- The SENCO has the opportunity to reassure the parent(s).
- A mutually agreed meeting can be arranged immediately.
- The SENCO is able to ask parents to consider particular factors and bring any appropriate information along to the meeting.

If there is no opportunity for speaking directly to the parent(s), contact should be made by letter. However, when writing for the first time about a child's learning difficulties careful consideration should be given to the wording of the letter. For this type of letter, and letters to invite parents into school to discuss progress, further concerns or pupil reviews, it is a good idea to use a pre-designed set if available. This will cut down the workload of the SENCO, particularly if there is an administrative assistant who is able to take on this task. (There is a sample set at the end of the chapter, Fig. 7.3.)

Having contacted the parent(s) and set up a meeting, the SENCO's role becomes all-important. Whether discussing initial concerns or the progress/performance of the child, there is a need for care and consideration. By providing a meeting area that is non-threatening the SENCO should endeavour to make the parent(s) feel at ease, encouraging them to talk freely about their child. The SENCO may also, where external agencies are involved, provide valuable support to the parent(s) who feels less than confident in those circumstances. If all of this can be achieved, the SENCO and the school will have the foundation for a fruitful partnership between themselves and the parent(s).

Wishing to take this further, in addition to meetings about learning and progress, I believe there is a great deal more that schools can offer to parents of pupils with SEN. For parents who have a child with a specific learning difficulty there are many support mechanisms that can be accessed for both the parents and the pupil. Schools can make the access to these much easier and indeed may develop their own. Links with parents are all-important and with this in mind, Figure 7.1 gives some ideas on areas that can be developed to build up strong positive links between home and school.

With a little hard work, if just a small number of these ideas come to fruition, the school will be able to provide a trusting caring environment in which the parent(s) feels a natural part of the school community.

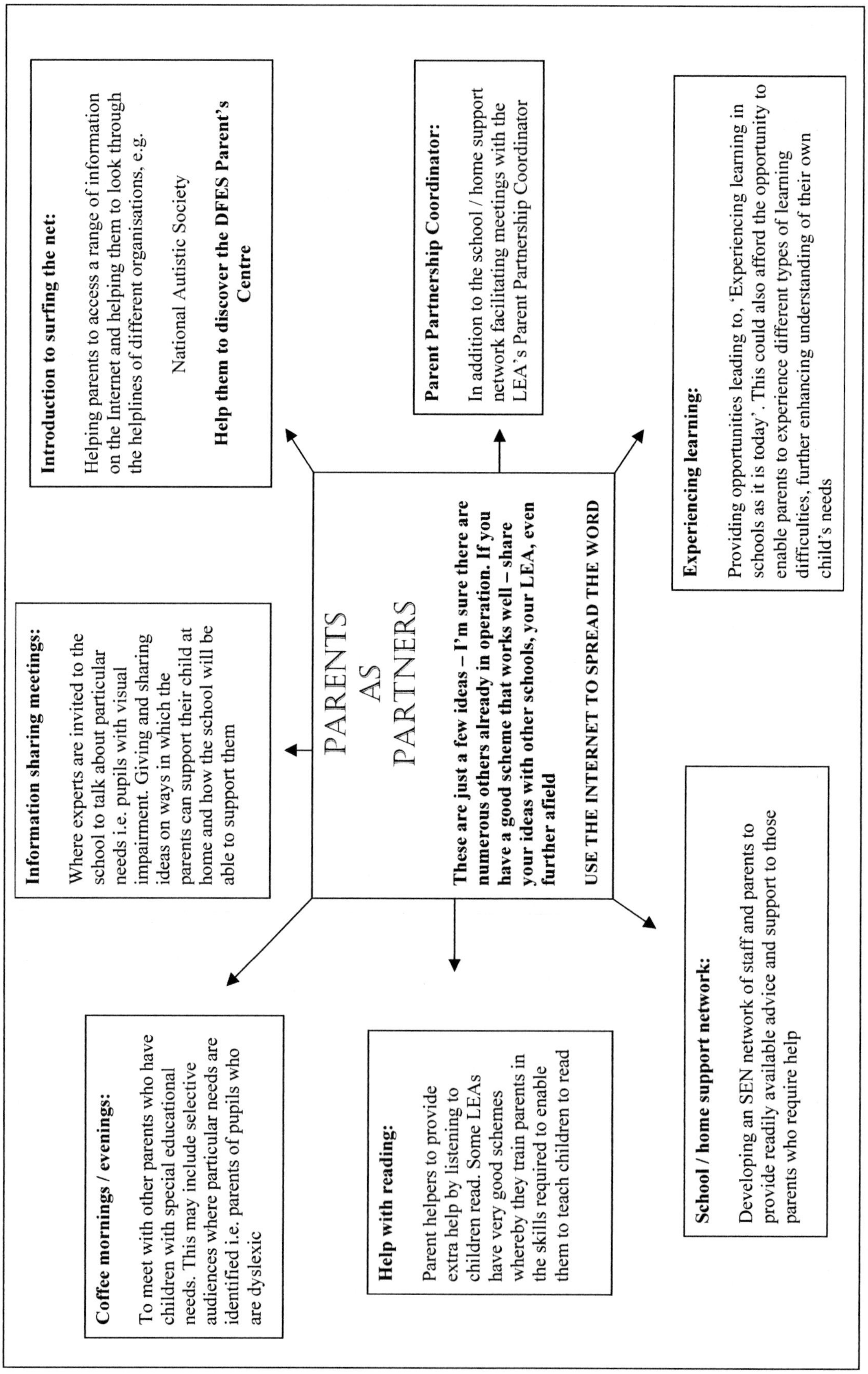
Coffee mornings / evenings:
To meet with other parents who have children with special educational needs. This may include selective audiences where particular needs are identified i.e. parents of pupils who are dyslexic
Help with reading:
Parent helpers to provide extra help by listening to children read. Some LEAs have very good schemes whereby they train parents in the skills required to enable them to teach children to read
School / home support network:
Developing an SEN network of staff and parents to provide readily available advice and support to those parents who require help
Information sharing meetings:
Where experts are invited to the school to talk about particular needs i.e. pupils with visual impairment. Giving and sharing ideas on ways in which the parents can support their child at home and how the school will be able to support them
PARENTS AS PARTNERS
These are just a few ideas – I'm sure there are numerous others already in operation. If you have a good scheme that works well – share your ideas with other schools, your LEA, even further afield
USE THE INTERNET TO SPREAD THE WORD
Introduction to surfing the net:
Helping parents to access a range of information on the Internet and helping them to look through the helplines of different organisations, e.g.
National Autistic Society
Help them to discover the DFES Parent's Centre
Parent Partnership Coordinator:
In addition to the school / home support network facilitating meetings with the LEA's Parent Partnership Coordinator
Experiencing learning:
Providing opportunities leading to, 'Experiencing learning in schools as it is today'. This could also afford the opportunity to enable parents to experience different types of learning difficulties, further enhancing understanding of their own child's needs

Copyright © 2002 Dot Constable, *Planning and Organising the SENCO Year*, ISBN 1 85346 802 9, published by David Fulton Publishers

Figure 7.1 Parents as partners – developing links between home and school

Working with external agencies

> Maintained schools **must** publish information that includes the school's arrangements for working in partnership with LEA support services, health and social services, the Connexions Service and any relevant local and national voluntary organisations. (DfES 2001: 10:1)

This statement highlights the legal requirement on schools to provide information on the external agencies with whom they are involved. It does not, however, suggest how that information is presented. The most logical place for a list of external agencies is contained in the school's SEN policy, but it should be just a matter of indicating which agencies rather than providing extensive information – this can be kept in school for reference purposes.

Where LEA services/contacts, social services, health services and the Connexions Service are concerned, contact numbers displayed and readily accessible are extremely helpful. Taking the time and effort where possible to discover a contact name for each department certainly provides speedier access. This type of contact will most certainly make the accessing of support an easier task and will, in turn, promote strong professional relationships. In addition to these services, contact names for voluntary organisations may be added when their input/support is required. The service provided by them is invaluable.

Having established a network of contacts the SENCO has, at hand, a wide variety of specialists to access. These should be considered both at School Action and School Action Plus. The Code of Practice points out:

> It is most likely that schools will consult specialists when they take action on behalf of a child through *School Action Plus*. But the involvement of specialists need not be limited to children receiving provision through *School Action Plus*. Outside specialists can play an important part in the very early identification of special educational needs and in advising schools on effective provision designed to prevent the development of more significant needs. They can act as consultants and be a source for in-service advice on learning and behaviour management strategies for all teachers. (DfES 2001: 10:13)

This is most definitely sound advice. Trying to 'peel off the layers', so to speak, to discover the true underlying SEN of older pupils can be a major task. I have lost count of the number of children I have dealt with during my career who have been referred for behavioural reasons when in fact, upon assessment, they have been identified as having a specific learning difficulty. I appeal to all schools to use the services available. Their mechanisms for observing and assessing pupils who are giving cause for concern when the school is unable to have a positive impact upon their learning is often an underused resource. No one can be an expert in all areas. No one school should expect to be able to identify all SEN. When in doubt, pick up the phone! LEA support networks are an excellent starting point – if they do not have the resources to support the school they will most certainly have information on further points of contact. LEAs are able to provide a range of services, some of which are shown in Figure 7.2. These support services are vital.

LEA Support

LEAs are allowed to hold centrally part of the government's funding allocation for SEN in order to provide:

Educational Psychology Service

A team of educational psychologists provides assessment, advice and support to schools on pupils who have been identified as having special educational needs. (Pupils at School Action Plus and those who are statemented will require specialised psychological testing at some point.)

Statement Administration

The LEA's SEN Administration Office initiates, collates and completes all paperwork required for formal assessment, writing of statements and statement reviews.

School/Pupil Support

Advice is given to schools on how to support SEN pupils at School Action. At School Action Plus in addition to the above the support services may be involved in working with individual pupils to complete assessments, monitor progress and possibly provide individual support.

Support services for pupils with visual, hearing or speech and language difficulties or other communication disorders including autism

Specialised teams will provide advice and support for those pupils who have specific learning difficulties and may require specialised resources or additional help in schools to enable them to access the curriculum effectively.

Promoting inclusion

LEAs work with mainstream and special schools to promote inclusion and provide opportunities for inter-school cooperation and working.

Large pupil-specific costs

There may be some pupils who require costly specialised equipment in order to function effectively in school.

Parent partnership schemes

LEAs provide parent partnership schemes to help those who require support or guidance on dealing with their child's special needs for example, guiding them through the statementing procedure, attending meetings with the school/LEA, accessing information from voluntary agencies etc.

Monitoring of SEN

The LEA SEN Advisory/Inspection Service will monitor SEN provision in all of its maintained schools.

Figure 7.2 LEA support

Moving on from this point, where children are referred to their LEA for formal assessment, a multi-agency working relationship becomes central to the process. It is a requirement of the Code of Practice for both social services and the local health authority to be involved alongside the LEA's own services. Their involvement continues if a statement of SEN is written. If this is the case, at the point of the annual review, all agencies involved are required to provide at least a written report and, where appropriate, to attend the review meeting. Consideration must also be given to the partnership between the LEA and the parent(s) – the SENCO of a school may well be the lynchpin between the two, being familiar with both parties.

Once a child has been issued with a statement, there is a need for a continuum of support from all parties concerned. This support should aim to be collective and as the Code of Practice points out:

> The objective should be to provide integrated, high quality, holistic support focused on the needs of the child. Such provision should be based on a shared perspective and should build wherever possible on mutual understanding and agreement. Services should adopt a flexible child-centred approach to service delivery to ensure that the changing needs of the child and their parents can be met at any given time. (DfES 2001: 10:4)

The focus here is rightly the 'child-centred' approach. If schools and outside agencies are to achieve this then there is a requirement by all to ensure joint meetings take place. The outcomes of such meetings should be the formulation of strategies and plans for support that do indeed have the best interests of the child at heart. Achieving this type of relationship is by no means an easy task – even arranging a meeting time that is suitable to all concerned may prove difficult. If this does prove to be a problem, those agencies not attending must at least be consulted. They should be asked for a written report and to provide recommendations for consideration. If this is achieved there will at least be a true multi-agency response to assessing and providing for an individual pupil's SEN.

Can all of these partnerships be achieved?

Experience has taught me that whatever objectives are laid down in front of schools from the 'powers that be', on the whole they achieve them. Since the inception of the original Code of Practice (DfEE 1994a) this has certainly been the case. Major steps have been taken in improving the provision for pupils with SEN. In the revised Code (DfES 2001), new chapters appear on working in partnership with parents and working in partnership with other agencies, both of which highlight the importance of collaborative working. I believe that, as in the past, these directives will be met and that this will once again benefit the children. It will, however, require a continuum of effort in order to be truly effective. Gathering a whole host of people and organisations together will never be an easy task. I envisage the SENCO playing a central role in its success. If this is the case, once again, good organisation and support will be vital to them.

SAMPLE LETTERS

FIRST CONTACT

Dear ……………

…………… seems to be having some difficulty with some of his / her work in school. I feel that a little extra support would help and I would like to talk to you about it.

I would very much like to meet you so that we can discuss the best way to help ………… achieve to the best of his / her ability. If …………. has had any help in the past, could you bring any information that you have along to the meeting as it may be useful.

I would appreciate it if you could telephone school to talk about the best time for a meeting to suit you.

I look forward to hearing from you.

Yours sincerely

………………

SENCO

LOW ACHIEVEMENT / POOR BEHAVIOUR / DISAFFECTION

Dear ……………

I would welcome the opportunity to discuss ……….'s progress in school at the moment.

…………… has shown he / she is capable of working well; however, this is not happening consistently across all subject areas. I feel that with support from both school and home this situation could be improved to the benefit of ………….

I would very much appreciate it if you would contact school to arrange an appointment to discuss this further. This would give us the opportunity to sit down with …………. and talk about a programme of action that would benefit him / her and enable …………… to achieve his / her full potential.

I look forward to hearing from you.

Signed by SENCO / Head of Year / Deputy Head according to responsibilities in school.

Figure 7.3a Sample letters

SAMPLE LETTERS

IEP REVIEW MEETING

Dear ....

I would like to invite you to a review meeting that has been arranged for (day) (date) at (time).

If you arrive at the school office on that day one of the office staff will take you to where the meeting is to be held. At the meeting we can discuss ....'s progress both in school and at home and set new targets for improvement.

If this date is not suitable please let us know so that another time can be arranged.

I look forward to hearing from you in the near future.

Yours sincerely

....

SENCO

STATEMENT REVIEW MEETING

Dear.............

.............'s annual statement review has been organised for (date) at (time). If you arrive at the school office on that day one of the office staff will take you to where the meeting is to be held.

It would be appreciated if you could complete the sheet enclosed with this letter to give your views on ....'s progress and return it to school by (day) (date). You will receive a copy of all information regarding his / her review the week before the date of the meeting.

At the meeting ....'s progress will be discussed, comments noted and along with all information gathered the written record of the review will be returned to the LEA within 5 days. The LEA will then notify you of its response.

If you are unable to attend the meeting at that time please contact the school immediately so that an alternative may be arranged.

I trust this meets with your approval and look forward to hearing from you.

Yours sincerely,

....

SENCO

Figure 7.3b Sample letters

8 The role and responsibilities of the SENCO as a manager

The role of the SENCO is clearly defined in the Code of Practice. It lays down guidelines towards what the designated person may be required to do and gives a good starting point for exploring the SENCO's role as a manager. Clear expectations are set out as to what the job could entail and in light of this, consideration should be given to the following points when establishing such roles and responsibilities.

- The development of the school's SEN policy.
- The day-to-day operation of the SEN policy.
- Raising the achievement of pupils with SEN.
- The record-keeping for those children with SEN.
- The coordination of SEN provision.
- Facilitating a collaborative working relationship with staff, parents and external agencies.
- Providing professional guidance to enable high quality teaching for children with SEN.
- Developing effective ways of overcoming barriers to learning for children with SEN.
- Sustaining effective teaching through the analysis and assessment of children's needs by monitoring teaching and standards of pupils' achievements.
- Working collaboratively with curriculum/literacy/numeracy coordinators to ensure equal opportunities for children with SEN.

When scanning through the list quickly it may not seem extensive but believe me, as one who has done the job – it is. The Code clearly take this into account emphasising both the importance of the managerial aspects of the role and the extent of the workload:

Experience shows that SENCOs require time for: planning and coordination away from the classroom; maintaining appropriate records including a record of children at *School Action* and *School Action Plus* and those with statements; teaching pupils with SEN; observing pupils in class without a teaching commitment; managing, supporting and training Learning Support Assistants;

liaising with colleagues and with early education settings and secondary schools. Access to a telephone and an interview room is also desirable where possible. In many schools the governing body has been able to allocate some administrative staff time to help the SENCO, thus releasing the SENCO to use their expertise more effectively. (DfES 2001: 5:33)

Where secondary colleagues are concerned, the advice also includes – 'managing effective deployment of other teachers within the SEN Team and liaising with departmental and pastoral colleagues; liaising with feeder primary schools and working with the Connexions Personal Adviser in relation to transition planning' (DfES 2001: 6:36).

There are two points for consideration here. First is the implications for head teachers and governing bodies for, whether the roles and responsibilities of the SENCO are shared, as in some schools they are, there is the need to enable the management of SEN to be effective. This can be done by providing, as suggested, sufficient time and adequate resources for carrying out the duties above. The second point is the actual work to be carried out and, irrespective of the first point, is something that needs to be done if SEN provision is to be successful. So, we ask ourselves, what can be done?

In respect of the first point it is unrealistic to expect SENCOs to be able to force action or impose change upon the powers that be, and it is therefore left for the managers of schools to decide what is best for their own institution. I would, however, suggest it would serve the managers well to consider the Code's emphasis on the use of the SENCO's expertise, particularly in relation to best value.

Where point two is concerned, there is definitely more that can be done. It is here that we move back to the main theme of the book, planning and organising. By looking at ideas, resources and systems it is possible to develop a streamlined structure in which the SENCO can work. I would at this point like to emphasise that no one can be a 'super SENCO' and that dependent on time allocation, SENCOs should make a conscious and realistic decision on how much they can carry out while remaining effective. 'Tis best to do less and achieve more than to do more and achieve less'!

With this in mind let us move on to look at the managerial role.

What to consider?

During the course of the book, consideration has been given to the areas of responsibility in respect of SEN, to suggestions on how to organise them, to ideas and paperwork to support appropriate systems and how they can be put in place. We have also taken into account working with children and adults in a variety of settings and ways. What we have not taken account of fully is, once the organisation is complete and the daily practice is taking place, how do we know our SEN provision is effective? What proof do we have? Do we have a system for evaluation and quality control?

Where to start?

Part 11 of the Foreword contained in the Code of Practice (DfES 2001) states:

Monitoring the SEN Code of Practice

The operation of Part IV of the 1996 Act, including the effect of this Code, will be closely monitored. Ofsted inspectors will look closely at schools' SEN policies and practices and through their examination of and reports on the education system, they will also monitor and evaluate the impact of this Code and other measures on schools and LEAs, including, for example, the impact of special educational needs support services. The Secretary of State will consider, in the light of this evaluation and all other relevant factors, whether and when the Code should be revised again.

This statement gives a very clear message to schools and LEAs that their provision for pupils with SEN will be under close scrutiny by Ofsted inspection teams. Taking this into account, at a school level, the SENCO must formulate processes, systems and practices to enable their school, on inspection, to demonstrate effective practice and provision for all aspects of SEN. With this in mind, as a SENCO I would want to provide sound evidence that the following was actively in place:

- Up-to-date policy documentation.
- Development plans.
- Organisation of provision.
- IEPs.
- Up-to-date records including pupil files.
- Evidence of pupil progress.
- SEN in the classroom.
- An inclusive approach by all, throughout the school.
- Funding/value for money.
- Evidence of constructive evaluation of all of the above.

To achieve this there is a need for a cycle of monitoring, evaluation, review and planning that is able to take into account changes affecting SEN provision. The nature and range of the difficulties faced by the children differ from year to year, staff turnover impacts upon pupils' learning and the allocation of the annual budget affects resourcing. These are just some of the factors that need careful thought. If SENCOs are to cater for such changes they must have a system in place that allows future planning to be constructive and applicable, and allows for a continuum of improvement to be realised. The question is, what sort of monitoring will provide the appropriate information required to carry this out?

What needs to be monitored?

Figure 8.1 (p. 82) outlines the areas the SENCO should consider monitoring. It provides a list of questions designed to encourage thought about the type of information required for evaluation purposes. Schools wishing to provide evidence of best value need to go through this type of process. In order to do this, we must consider how the evidence may be assimilated and by what methods.

Finding the evidence and evaluating its effectiveness

Let us turn to Figure 8.2 (p. 83) which outlines evidence bases that could provide the information required for evaluation purposes. When looking at the diagram keep firmly in the back of your mind what is already in place. By taking this into account it will soon become apparent that a great deal of the work may already have been completed. Where paperwork is concerned, proof is readily available both from observation and by questioning – is it there? Can we see it? Do we know what it is for? Is it used?

The difficulty arises when we move towards evaluating practice. Once again it is a matter for observation and questioning but at this point, careful consideration needs to be given because interpersonal skills become all-important. Whether it is by lesson observation or just a matter of discussion, those involved must not feel threatened by the process; it is imperative that the feeling created should be one of mutual support that in turn enables best practice to be achieved.

With this in mind, the lesson observation proforma was created (Fig. 8.3a, b, pp. 87, 88). It centres on post-lesson discussion where positive feedback may be given and suggestions for improvement can be shared. It also provides the opportunity for appropriate support to be offered to either teacher or pupil(s) from both subject and pastoral areas where a referral is indicated. It focuses heavily on the strategies required for effective teaching and learning for those pupils with SEN. At the same time it encourages the observer to identify those pupils who are not engaged in learning and asks the all-important question – why? Finally, it asks the observer to comment on the effectiveness of learning support during the lesson.

Completing this type of lesson observation proforma will provide a suitable evidence base to enable evaluation of a range of SEN issues:

• Was the lesson accessible to pupils with SEN?
• Was provision in place for those pupils who on their IEP had particular type(s) of support noted?
• Were all noted resources available/in use?
• Did appropriate assessment of learning take place?
• Were the pupils able to achieve to the best of their ability?

These are goals schools must look towards achieving if they are to enable effective teaching and learning for those pupils with SEN.

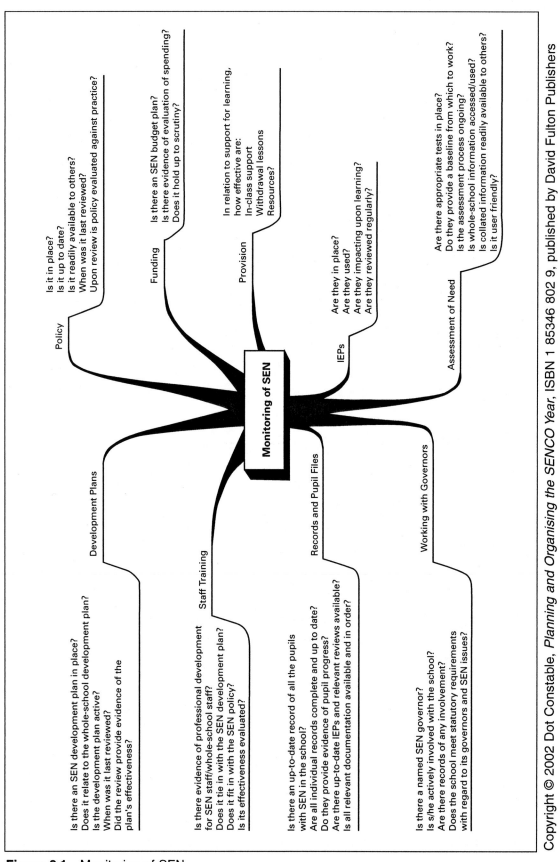

Figure 8.1 Monitoring of SEN

Evidence for the Evaluation of SEN Provision

PAPERWORK IN PLACE

SEN paperwork:

- SEN policy
- Development plan
- Record of pupils with SEN (register)
- IEPs
- Pupil records
- Assessment information
- Record of allocated support
- Lesson records for all learning support
- SEN spending plan
- School policies with reference to SEN i.e. subject areas, pastoral areas
- Governor reports including statutory annual report

PRACTICE IN PLACE

SEN policy works in practice by providing:

- IEPs for all designated SEN pupils
- Pupil reviews
- Learning support – in-class, withdrawal
- Resources
- Staff training
- SEN governor monitoring and statutory reports
- Ongoing assessment of pupils
- Collation of information and distribution to all concerned

Checking it out by:

Observation:

- Looking at the paperwork – does it exist? Is it in place?
- Seeing if information on IEPs is evident / being used
- Watching lessons – are pupils accessing the curriculum? Are their needs catered for? Is designated support apparent?
- Analysis of comparative data in relation to pupil progress

Questioning:

- Asking if appropriate paperwork has been received, is in place – is it working and achieving its purpose?
- Talking to staff, children, parents and outside agencies about their perceptions of the SEN provision in place and progress being made
- Receiving verbal and written feedback from a variety of sources e.g. parents' evenings, school meetings, external agencies etc.

Figure 8.2 Evidence for the evaluation of SEN provision

I hope that we are now at the point where there is enough information for SENCOs to feel comfortable with monitoring and evaluating their SEN provision. I do not, however, intend to leave it at this point. There are some issues that are equally important to those already covered that have not, at some point, been dealt with adequately.

The SEN development plan

This needs to be considered as a rolling programme to allow for short-, medium- and long-term objectives. It should also take into account the whole-school development plan where it impacts upon SEN provision. The aim of the plan is to provide for a continuum of improvement but the question is, from this point on, where do we start? Have faith, it isn't as difficult as it seems. It is possible to approach the task in a very systematic and logical way. The following points will provide the information required to facilitate effective planning:

- Numbered objectives (cross-referenced to the school development plan where possible/appropriate).
- A separate plan of action for each objective.
- The person responsible for carrying out the action plan.
- Criteria for success.
- Target date for completion.
- Who is to monitor it.
- How it is to be evaluated.
- What resources will be needed to carry out the action plan.
- The cost of the action carried out.

The proforma (Fig. 8.4, p. 89) shows a format that is used, in some form, by a number of schools. It encompasses all of the above points and sets out an expectation for the monitoring and evaluating of SEN provision. It also allows for highlighting, on paper, a range of tasks to be carried out by specified personnel thus establishing some degree of accountability. This at times can be most helpful in supporting the SENCO when it comes to delegation.

In-service training

I cannot emphasise strongly enough the need to ensure that all staff are appropriately trained with regard to SEN issues. I would suggest that where schools are unsure about what training is required, the initial movement should be an audit of training to discover the SEN expertise within the school that already exists, the differing needs of the pupils and the differing needs of the staff. From this information future training needs can be identified and prioritised. This part of the process does not necessarily have to be carried out by the SENCO alone. It should be discussed with the member of staff in charge of professional development as the outcomes of the audit will most definitely have funding implications.

Once the audit has been completed and a training programme has been decided upon we are back to evaluation and best value. In order to demonstrate this there is a need for those who have attended training to provide information on the following:

- The training received.
- Who delivered it.
- The total cost.
- Who benefited from the training.
- Has it had an impact on the pupils?
- Has it improved practice within the school?

This should not be seen as an onerous task and may be done relatively easily by simple record-keeping forms that can be collated to provide an overall picture of the SEN professional development (see Figs 8.5a,b,c,d, pp. 90–93). Remember this does not have to be the sole responsibility of the SENCO, and once again I return to the value of an administrative assistant who could in fact collate all of the information for both the SENCO and the member of staff in charge of professional development.

Working with the SEN governor

Governing bodies have statutory duties that outline their responsibilities with regard to SEN provision within a school. These include:

- Reporting annually to parents on the school's SEN policy and its implementation.
- Having regard to the Code of Practice when carrying out its duties towards all pupils with SEN.
- Ensuring parents are notified when the school decides to make SEN provision for their child.

Governors should also ensure that:

- they are fully involved in developing and monitoring the school's SEN policy
- they are knowledgeable about the school's SEN provision including deployment of funding, equipment, personnel and resources
- SEN is an integral part of the whole-school development plan
- the quality of SEN is continually monitored.

The message implicit in all of the above is the role of the governing body in monitoring and evaluating the school's SEN provision. This is often a delegated responsibility whereby one person is asked to take on the role of SEN governor, although some schools do have a sub-committee to carry out the designated duties. Whatever the system there are implications for the school, the SENCO and the designated person(s). I would suggest the most effective way forward would be to develop a strong working relationship that encourages the sharing of information, the opportunity for independent monitoring and the capability for working towards shared goals. What is imperative in all of this, however, is that whatever the involvement, it must not impinge on the organisation and running of the school's day-to-day SEN provision.

Some local authorities provide good training that enhances the governor's knowledge of SEN and provides ideas for themselves and the school for carrying out their duties effectively. It would serve SENCOs well to investigate what is available within their own LEA. Remember – we are looking to lighten the load so, any appropriate external help should be readily sought.

Time management

This is probably the most difficult area to deal with as there often seems so much to do and not enough time to do it. Most managers come up against this problem but there are no hard and fast solutions; organising one's own time is a very individual and personal thing. But, take care, poor time management can double the workload. What I would like to offer on a positive note is the following:

PLAN AHEAD

HAVE A WEEKLY DIARY

USE THE YEARLY PLANNER

SPREAD OUT PRESSURE POINTS

DELEGATE WHEREVER YOU CAN

GET ADMINISTRATIVE ASSISTANCE

PRACTISE SAYING THE WORD NO!

It sums up my advice succinctly and, if taken, I have no doubt will definitely impact on relieving stress and pressure!

At this point, I hope I have covered the important aspects of the roles and responsibilities of the SENCO. I trust that I have provided some help and assistance and that in some way the duties and tasks involved with the job may seem a little less daunting.

SEN Monitoring Form

Date:_____ Lesson:_____ Class/Year Group:_____

Teacher:_____ Support Teacher:_____

Class Ability: Mixed ☐   Banded ☐   Streamed ☐

No. on SEN Stages: School Action ☐ School Action Plus ☐ Statemented ☐

Context of the lesson: _____

_____

_____

Classroom Management and Organisation	Strategy Used	Strategy Suggested
Classroom well organised and seating considered		
Positive attitude to learning established		
Use of routine to start lesson		
Make objectives clear/visible		
Make tasks clear/visible		
Have spare writing equipment available		
Resources readily available		
Make sure rewards, sanctions and rules are understood and applied consistently		
Teaching and Learning		
Make instructions/explanations clear specific and easily understood		
Use repetition and review during lesson		
Give choice of tasks		
Give choice of outcomes		
Give vocabulary to be used		
Teach KEYWORDS		
Display KEYWORDS		
Individual/small group and whole-class teaching		
Extra time to complete tasks		
Use visual aids/cues		
Use practical/tactile activities		
Reading materials – suitable for whole class		
– modified		
– allow peer support		
– give individual support		
– supported by pictures/graphics		
– sufficient copies		
– size of print appropriate		
Use appropriate strategies to teach spelling		
Use appropriate strategy to teach reading of unknown words		
Use ICT		
Assessment		
Uses school assessment policy		
Uses formal and informal assessment		
Sets targets for improvement		

Figure 8.3a Lesson observation proforma

Name of pupil not on task	Reasons e.g. poor behaviour, not accessing curriculum, SEN	Refer to Subject	Refer to Pastoral

Effectiveness of support:

Completed by: Date:

Designation:

Figure 8.3b Lesson observation proforma

SEN DEVELOPMENT PLAN										
No.	Objective	Plan of Action	Person Responsible	Success Criteria	Target Date	Monitored	Evaluation	Resources	Costs Involved
1									
2									
3									
4									

Figure 8.4   Sample SEN development plan

Audit for Training

Complete the boxes to establish the training needs for SEN

List the SEN expertise that exists in the school:

List the differing needs of the pupils:

List the needs of the staff in respect of SEN issues:

Use the information to identify future training needs:

From the identified list prioritise the first five in order of importance and indicate who is to deliver i.e. names of school staff or external providers:

Figure 8.5a SEN professional development – training pack

Inset Evaluation

Name: .... Department: ....

Title of course/training: ....

Brief description of course content: ....
....
....
....
....

How effective was the training: ....
....
....
....
....

Is the training to be disseminated? If so, where and how: ....
....
....
....
....

From the above please answer the following:

Value for money. Has the training been of benefit to

		Yes	No
You?		☐	☐
SEN Staff?		☐	☐
Whole School:	Staff?	☐	☐
	Pupils?	☐	☐

Signed: .... Date: ....

Figure 8.5b   SEN professional development – training pack

Inventory of Staff Receiving SEN Training

Name: _____

Designation: _____

Title of Course: _____

Date of Course: _____

Purpose of the course – e.g. pupil-led/school-led need:

Evaluation of Course:

☐ Fulfilled expectations of participant   ☐ Was gauged as good value for money

☐ Has had an impact on pupil(s)   ☐ Has changed practice in school

---

Name: _____

Designation: _____

Title of Course: _____

Date of Course: _____

Purpose of the course – e.g. pupil-led/school-led need:

Evaluation of Course:

☐ Fulfilled expectations of participant   ☐ Was gauged as good value for money

☐ Has had an impact on pupil(s)   ☐ Has changed practice in school

---

Name: _____

Designation: _____

Title of Course: _____

Date of Course: _____

Purpose of the course – e.g. pupil-led/school-led need:

Evaluation of Course:

☐ Fulfilled expectations of participant   ☐ Was gauged as good value for money

☐ Has had an impact on pupil(s)   ☐ Has changed practice in school

---

Name: _____

Designation: _____

Title of Course: _____

Date of Course: _____

Purpose of the course – e.g. pupil-led/school-led need:

Evaluation of Course:

☐ Fulfilled expectations of participant   ☐ Was gauged as good value for money

☐ Has had an impact on pupil(s)   ☐ Has changed practice in school

Figure 8.5c   SEN professional development – training pack

Record of SEN Training				
Name	Date of Training	Purpose of Training	Effective	Ineffective

Figure 8.5d   SEN professional development – training pack

9 Conclusion

If you listen to any group of SENCOs chatting they might for a few minutes talk or indeed moan about their latest frustrations or problems, but I can guarantee that before the conversation ends they are merrily talking about the children in their care. The stories of working with particular pupils bring much sought after light relief as with smiles they recall the latest happenings. That is the one of the great rewards of working with children who have SEN. No matter how hard life gets each day there is always something that acts as a reminder as to why it is so worthwhile. Unfortunately what it can't do is take away the tiredness and exhaustion that results from the stresses, strains and demands of the managerial aspects of the work.

From the outset, the intention of this publication was to support SENCOs in their efforts towards achieving a sustainable, manageable workload, as for many this at some point or other in their career may well prove to be difficult. These are the times when the proverbial spinning of the plates comes to mind – I know because I've been there!

In the Introduction I pointed out the numerous tasks that can be active at any one time and that, in order to survive, good strategic planning was vital. At the same time, however, I emphasised that SEN is a whole-school issue and in light of this, implicit throughout the book, I hope, has been the message to managers of schools about their role in supporting/facilitating effective SEN provision. Everyone in the school must have a sound understanding and work together with a common goal in mind – to provide equal opportunities for those pupils with SEN.

When establishing the format of the book I decided that I should base it around the requirements of the Code of Practice (DfES 2001) and the Teacher Training Agency (TTA) *National Standards for Special Educational Needs Coordinators* (TTA 1998). After considering both and being mindful of the duties and responsibilities laid down in respect of the SENCO I set out to achieve the following:

- To give guidance on the development of appropriate policy and other relevant documentation.
- To provide examples/guidance for good strategic planning.
- To promote good quality SEN provision.

94

- To enhance the SENCO's ability to carry out their role including their ability to monitor, evaluate and develop plans for improvement.
- To save time by providing adaptable strategies/ideas/resources throughout.

Like any good teacher, it is at this point of the book that I review my goals and hope that I have realised them. At no point do I expect it to meet all of the reader's needs but, if it has only served to raise awareness and establish a pattern of re-evaluation, it will certainly have been worthwhile. For those of you embarking on your career as a SENCO for the first time, my wishes are that it may at least act as a support mechanism and answer some of the questions you could face. For those that it can't answer, my advice is don't worry – there are many talented and experienced SENCOs out there, seek them out and ask for their help. I am sure they will be only too pleased to respond.

Finally, as I move towards a conclusion, I would like to point out that all of the ideas in this book have come about from the desire to build effective SEN provision. They have arisen from the needs of the children in my care and the search to find ways of supporting their learning. Over a number of years they may have been refined in some way at the same time as new ideas coming on board. Time does not stand still and we should be mindful that there is a constant need to re-evaluate and adapt to change. If we can do this, I am confident we can support the children in our care and provide an inclusive environment in which they are able to live and work in harmony and have the opportunity to achieve their full potential, for this is surely what we are all working towards.

References and further reading

References

Department for Education and Employment (DfEE) (1994a) *The Code of Practice on the Identification and Assessment of Pupils with Special Educational Needs*. London: DfEE.

Department for Education and Employment (DfEE) (1994b) Circular 6/94, *The Organisation of Special Educational Provision*. London: DfEE.

Department for Education and Employment (DfEE) (1997) *Excellence for All Children: Meeting Special Educational Needs*. London: DfEE.

Department for Education and Employment (DfEE) (1998) *Meeting Special Educational Needs: A Programme of Action*. London: DfEE.

Department for Education and Skills (DfES) (2001) *Special Educational Needs: Code of Practice*. London: The Stationery Office.

HMSO (2001) *Special Educational Needs and Disability Act 2001*. London: HMSO.

Teacher Training Agency (TTA) (1998) *National Standards for Special Educational Needs Coordinators*. London: TTA.

Further reading

Cheminais, Rita (2000) *Special Educational Needs for Newly Qualified Teachers – A Practical Guide*. London: David Fulton Publishers.

Department for Education and Employment (DfEE) (1997) *The SENCO Guide*. London: DfEE.

Drummond, Mary Jane (1993) *Assessing Children's Learning*. London: David Fulton Publishers.

Garner, Philip and Davies, John Dwyfor (2001) *Introducing Special Educational Needs – A Guide for Students*. London: David Fulton Publishers.

Headington, Rita (2000) *Monitoring, Assessment, Recording, Reporting and Accountability – Meeting the Standards*. London: David Fulton Publishers.

Landy, Maria and Gains, Charles (1996) *Inspecting Special Needs Provision in Schools*. London: David Fulton Publishers.

Lindsay, Geoff and Desforges, Martin (1998) *Baseline Assessment – Practice, Problems and Possibilities*. London: David Fulton Publishers.

Lorenz, Stephanie (1998) *Effective In-Class Support – The Management of Support Staff in Mainstream and Special Schools*. London: David Fulton Publishers.

Mittler, Peter (2000) *Working Towards Inclusive Education – Social Contexts*. London: David Fulton Publishers.

Office for Standards in Education (Ofsted) (1999a) *The SEN Code of Practice Three Years on. The Contribution of Individual Education Plans to the Raising of Standards for Pupils with Special Educational Needs*. London: Ofsted.

Office for Standards in Education (Ofsted) (1999b) *Inspecting Schools. Handbook for Inspecting Primary and Nursery Schools*. London: The Stationery Office.

Office for Standards in Education (Ofsted) (1999c) *Inspecting Schools. Handbook for Inspecting Schools*. London: The Stationery Office.

Wolfendale, Sheila and Einzig, Hetty (1999) *Parenting Education and Support – New Opportunities*. London: David Fulton Publishers.

Index

Printed in the United Kingdom
by Lightning Source UK Ltd.
112735UKS00001B/311